Christian Maclagan

Frontispiece *Mither Tap o'Bennachie: members of Hillforts Study Group (Ian Ralston; Bob Hogg; Ken Smith; Graeme Guilbert and Offa the dog; Trevor Cowie; Ian Shepherd; David Longley et al) examine the remains of the entrance to the fort, April 1981*

Christian Maclagan

Stirling's formidable
lady antiquary

SHEILA M ELSDON

ΧΡΙΣΤΙΑΝ

The Pinkfoot Press

Balgavies, Angus
2004

Published 2004 in Scotland by
The Pinkfoot Press
Balgavies, Forfar, Angus DD8 2TH

ISBN 1 874012 43 1

Designed and typeset at The Pinkfoot Press
Printed by The Cromwell Press, Trowbridge

In memory of my husband Konrad who made me persevere.

Contents

List of Illustrations

Acknowledgements

The initial impulse for this book came from John Harrison, a historical researcher based in Stirling. He discovered that Stirling Library held a collection of colour slides of Christian Maclagan's 'rubbings' of Christian gravestones and, at the same time, found a letter of mine enquiring about them. I knew of the existence of the slides, made by Miss I R Williams of Ohio, but did not know their present whereabouts. I am enormously indebted to Miss Williams for what must have been a mammoth task of taking the excellent colour transparencies and to the staff of Stirling Libraries Archive Deparment, Elma Lindsay and Sheila Miller, who allowed me to view them and arranged for prints of a few chosen examples in this volume. As I do not know Miss Williams's current address I have been unable to thank her personally but her generous donation of the whole set to Stirling Library is of great value to historical researchers.

Steve Dowman and the staff of Stirling Library have been very supportive in providing me with copies of obituaries, papers from the *Transactions of the Stirling Natural History and Archaeological Society* and with photocopies of parts of Miss Maclagan's books, as well as in assisting my searches of the Census returns. Elspeth King, Director of the Smith Art Gallery and Museum in Stirling has been most helpful and encouraging throughout, as has Graham Ritchie, formerly of the Royal Commission and expert on illustrations of Celtic and Pictish monuments. George Dixon and Alison Lindsay of the Archives Department of the Central Regional Council have helped with my fruitless searches for vanished material. Elma Lindsay kindly advised me on my historical research, Bill Cavanagh of Nottingham University Archaeology Department advised on the Nuraghi literature, and Roger Wilson also of Nottingham University helped and encouraged me.

The staff of the Royal Commission on Ancient and Historical Monuments of Scotland, in particular Iain Fraser and Miriam Macdonald kindly sorted out for me Miss Maclagan's original watercolours and drawings and allowed me the use of a recent survey of the Mither Tap o' Bennachie. Michelle Brown of the Manuscripts Department of the British Library facilitated my scrutiny of some of the originals of Miss Maclagan's 'rubbings' and gave permission for the reproduction here of some of Miss Williams's slides. The Librarian of the Iona Community generously supplied me with photocopies of five of the tombstones in the published corpus, and finally Morag Cross of Linlithgow shared with me some views on the 'women's angle' which she is currently researching.

David Henry of the Pinkfoot Press, one of the few people I have come across who has actually read Miss Maclagan's 'Catalogue Raisonné' of her rubbings, supplied me with interesting ideas as to why she made them and published them in the manner she did. The illustration of Christian Maclagan taking the rubbing at Fowlis Wester (**61**) is by Owain Kirby and the sonnet by James Robertson.

Undoubtedly the greatest assistance to my research was the extended loan, by the Society of Antiquaries of London, of their precious copy of Miss Maclagan's hillforts book. The convenience of having it at home for constant reference has been an enormous advantage.

Finally I want to thank my husband, Konrad, for encouraging me to write the book in the first place, enthusiastic help with the research, nagging me to make progress and for advice and help with the ordering and correction of the text.

December 2003   SME

1 *Canna: pencil drawing (Crown Copyright RCAHMS)*

Illustrations

The author gratefully acknowledges permission to reproduce illustrative material as follows: Royal Commission on the Ancient and Historical Monuments of Scotland (RCAHMS) (nos **1–3, 6–7, 32**); Smith Art Gallery and Museum, Stirling (**44–5**); Stirling Libraries, Courtesy of the British Library Board (**55–56a, 58–60, 62, 63c,d**); David Henry (**53, 64**); James Robertson and Owain Kirby (**60**)

2 *Dun Telve, Inverness-shire: interior view after Gordon (1726) (Crown Copyright RCAHMS)*

3 *Dun Troddan, Inverness-shire: interior view after Gordon (1726) (Crown Copyright RCAHMS)*

Introduction

Christian Maclagan was probably the earliest female archaeologist, in her own right, in the British Isles, and as such is a truly remarkable woman. Her career proper did not start until fairly late in life, when she was free of family responsibilities and had a comfortable income. However, as she was fortunate enough to live into her nineties in full possession of her faculties, she had ample time to make her mark in the archaeological world of her day. To the best of my knowledge there is no other Scottish or English lady archaeologist to equal her in the nineteenth century.

Yet today she is almost unknown and her work neglected even by specialists in her subject. There cannot be many people who merited an entry in the *Dictionary of National Biography* (*DNB*) the memory of whom has faded so surprisingly less than one hundred years after death. Moreover, although Christian Maclagan **is** remembered in the folk-memory of her home town of Stirling as a somewhat eccentric battle-axe of a woman, the importance of her archaeological work is largely forgotten or ignored. Even the manuscript autobiography, mentioned in the *DNB*, has disappeared, perhaps destroyed by family members embarrassed by its revelations. No photographs or even drawings of her appear to exist. The Stirling Natural History and Archaeological Society has portraits of almost all its gentleman members at the turn of the century; Maclagan does not figure athough she probably made a greater contribution to the archaeology of Scotland than almost any of her male contemporaries in that Society. This book is an attempt to rectify the situation; to assess the value of her neglected archaeological work and to draw attention to some of her unique, idiosyncratic and sometimes highly amusing ways of presenting her material.

Part of the reason for the neglect of Miss Maclagan's work and opinions in her own day could be that she clearly had an abrasive and very assertive personality of the kind that easily makes enemies and, at best, causes others to take evasive action. She was very well-read, had travelled widely, and had seen and measured (some cynics said with her umbrella) all of the monuments that she describes. She probably knew more than most antiquaries from first-hand experience and was never afraid to say so. Her conviction in the accuracy of her own observations was so much part and parcel of her sense of personal rectitude that she refused to entertain any contrary arguments. In some cases she may have slanted the evidence to prove her theories. It is quite possible to understand how such a woman would have antagonized others working in the field so that the true value of her work was submerged under a huge sigh of relief when she left the scene.

Today our interest lies in the background of someone who, by any standards, made a major contribution to archaeology in Scotland, but was deeply angered by the lack of respect and recognition paid to her by her peers which she reckoned was her due.

She was never admitted as a Fellow of the Society of Antiquaries of Scotland because of her sex. This was quite normal at the time, but she took it as a personal insult. She was a devout Free Church member who certainly knew her own worth. Why could not others appreciate it, although she was 'only a mere woman'?

If you visit the cemetery of the Church of the Holy Rude (Valley Cemetery) in Stirling and search diligently amongst the many elaborate tombs, you might notice an austere, polished, granite grave-slab with the simple inscription, in Greek, ΧΡΙΣΤΙΑΝ (see title-page). Next to it is a similar slab, but giving more information about the deceased it commemorates: *Janet Colville d.1858, wife of George Maclagan d.1818* (**4**). These are the graves of a mother and daughter. The gravestone for the mother was probably laid down by her daughter Christian, who requested in

4 *Valley Cemetery, Stirling: mother and daughter together in death (Photo: SME)*

her own will that an identical slab, with Greek inscription, should be put in place over her own grave. This concern about suitable memorial stones was common practice at the time when it was considered healthy to ponder ones own mortality. Who were these people and why the one enigmatic gravestone, the deceased's choice,

5 *Ravenscroft, Stirling, the house which Christian had built in 1858 (Photo: SME)*

but with no dates added subsequently? Was she afraid, quite correctly, that her reputation would not survive her death? The curious can visit her large house, *Ravenscroft*, which she had built in 1858 and, although now in multiple occupation, it stands in a still prosperous part of Stirling **(5)**. She lived there with her devoted companion, Jessie Colvin, and three female servants. Being a shrewd Scotswoman, she let out one half of the house. In her will, after having left very substantial legacies to friends, servants, associates and worthy causes, she left the rather meagre remains of what must at one time have been a not inconsiderable fortune, to a cousin on her mother's side. All her immediate relatives had predeceased her, including her close aide and companion, Miss Colvin, who died of pleurisy in 1890.

Christian Maclagan's life spanned ninety-two years (1809–1901). In the confines of her home town she was a well-known figure, especially as a devout churchwoman and philanthropist in the field of improving slum housing. Her wider reputation was considerable as a field archaeologist and recorder of Iron Age forts and brochs, and Christian Celtic crosses and Pictish symbol stones. She published profusely and in great detail on these subjects.

Her major publication was a huge tome entitled *The Hill Forts, Stone Circles, and other Structural Remains of Ancient Scotland* (1875) (hereafter *Hill Forts*), which is now virtually neglected. The profuse illustrations are all in her own hand. The book includes a complete gazetteer of all the monuments of these types in Scotland that were known at the time – possibly the first time that this had been done. Her second major contribution to posterity was a collection of over three hundred 'rubbings', of prehistoric, early medieval and medieval carved stones in Scotland, which are now deposited in the British Library in London. These are accompanied by extensive notes and again a complete published catalogue.

She contributed to the *Proceedings of the Society of Antiquaries of Scotland* (*PSAS*) and regularly to the *Transactions of the Stirling Natural History and Archaeological Society* (*Trans Stirling*) amongst other learned journals. She had four exhibitions of her 'rubbings', two at Glasgow and two at Stirling, which were warmly acclaimed and supported by eminent people, including Sir James Young Simpson, a prominent antiquarian but better known as the pioneer in the use of chloroform in childbirth and who attended Queen Victoria herself. Miss Maclagan was certainly not without an entourage of admiring clerical gentlemen who sometimes accompanied her on expeditions and corresponded regularly with her. Yet today, unlike many contemporary Victorian ladies, such as Mary Kingsley, Margaret Fountain, Florence Nightingale and Elizabeth Fry, who came into money and travelled widely, she is largely unknown. One of these women contemporaries came from a well-known literary family and fought off crocodiles with her umbrella; while another, wisely, did not allow access to her memoirs until fifty years after her death as she travelled widely with her Turkish dragoman and lover, who later turned out to be married with three children. One is tempted to speculate that adventures might have figured in Christian Maclagan's lost autobiography, which friends might not have thought fit to make public; or was it simply of no interest to them? Certainly in the 1861 census return, when she must have been 51 or 52, she gives her age as 47.

Part of the reason for her disappearance from the record may be that she was a woman of strong convictions who did not hesitate to mention them at every conceivable moment, and she made many enemies during her lifetime. She never forgave the Society of Antiquaries of Scotland for not admitting her as a Fellow, in spite of the fact that no women were admitted at that time. Christian Maclagan also had strong views on religious matters and a well-developed sense of social responsibility, which sometimes brought her into bitter conflict with the Free Church of Scotland and its powerful local Minister. Here was a character who was capable of making many enemies as well as many devoted and admiring friends of either sex.

Nevertheless it has to be admitted that her strongly held, if somewhat eccentric, views about the nobility and fortitude of the native Scottish people, and the nature of brochs and stone circles, coloured and sometimes corrupted her descriptions of antiquities, and must have aggravated her contemporaries, who noted her tendency to see a broch in every circular structure. She was formidable in argument, but also blessed with a good sense of humour at her own expense. And yet, even at the end of her long life she was looking forward to a future when she hoped that some of the motifs she had recorded from the Celtic crosses might inspire a new generation of artists. She was also an artist of 'no mean ability' as her pen and wash drawings and watercolours show. Some of these are preserved in the National Monuments Record of Scotland (NMRS) at the Royal Commission on the Ancient and Historical Monuments of Scotland (RCAHMS) in Edinburgh, in the collection of manuscripts deposited by the Society of Antiquaries of Scotland, and they show great sensitivity to landscape (eg **6**).

The list of Lady Associates of the Society of Antiquaries of Scotland for 1871 consists of four titled Ladies and two Misses. Miss Maclagan is one and the other is a Miss Stokes of Dublin. Margaret Stokes, who also merits an entry in the *DNB*, worked with George Petrie, for whom she illustrated his work on the High Crosses of Ireland and she also illustrated works by the Earl of Dunraven. Her earliest publication was in 1861 and the last in 1898. She too travelled abroad, to the Forests of France and to the Apennines in Italy in search of vestiges of Irish Saints. Unlike Christian, she used the new medium of photography to illustrate some of her books. These two could have known each other, but there seems to be no record, although a descendant of Miss Stokes is currently writing a biography. Would that there were such a devoted descendant of Christian Maclagan!

6 *Ballymeanach, Argyll: stone circles. A monochrome wash drawing by Christian (Crown Copyright RCAHMS)*

Surely the time has come for a reassessment of this remarkable lady and her contribution to archaeology, social and religious reform and the place of women in society. We now see her as misguided in some of her opinions and the victim, upon occasion, of her own enthusiastic beliefs. She was an important pioneer as a field archaeologist, working under conditions very different to those of today, who at least looked and recorded to the best of her ability and, through her publications, encouraged others to do so. Much of what she recorded is no longer visible after over a hundred years. Since her time many eminent women archaeologists have emerged, such as Kathleen Kenyon (Jericho, Breedon-on-the-Hill), Lily F Chitty (Shropshire and Wales), Elsie Clifford (Bagendon), Helen O'Neil (Scilly Isles, Gloucestershire etc) and later Margaret Jones (Mucking, Essex), who had the same fearful reputation as Christian's – renowned archaeologists quailed before her.

Here, then, was an archaeologist, a colourful public figure, a feminist, an ardent Scottish patriot and a 'character' who is well worth retrieving from oblivion.

1   Background – nineteenth-century Stirling

Christian Maclagan was fortunate to grow up in a period of great optimism and expansion, in which new discoveries and opportunities were frequent and almost anything must have seemed possible. There were opportunities for travel, for wealthy middle-class women at least, which had been restricted to the aristocracy in the previous century. The poor were numerous of course, and ever more obvious as they flocked to the towns for employment in the new industries, but, for those with a comfortable income, the world was opening up and was full of opportunities, even for women. There was a great feeling of optimism about the future. It is not surprising that Christian felt great hope for improvement in the conditions for women and was irritated at the slowness of progress in some areas.

Stirling was a smallish town in 1820 when Christian arrived there as a girl of about ten. (The population is given as 8,868 in the 1841 census). A late 1820s print of Broad Street, the main market street of the town and the thoroughfare leading up to the Castle gates, shows a street of compressed earth with heaps of rubbish, and women attempting primitive forms of washing clothes in the streams of water that were running down the road. In 1836, the streets were still hard-packed earth and stones and this was gradually replaced by cobbles. In winter they were a porridge of animal manure, dust and water. The 'crossings' were paved strips for pedestrians to cross over this mess; the sweepers were not paid, but depended on tips from the users. But as early as 1854, there was declared 'no deficiency of water in Stirling', which enabled the narrow closes that separated the overcrowded houses to be subjected to periodical cleaning. But the other side of the coin was that as late as 1893 houses at Plean, outside the main town, still had no rainwater drains, the streets were still compressed earth where rubbish was left in piles. What had gone wrong and why the inequality? Perhaps the houses at Plean were just miners' dwellings! These matters deeply concerned Christian, as did working and housing conditions for the labouring poor of the town itself.

The traditional industry was wool-weaving, particularly of tartan cloth, and there was a mill at Bannockburn as early as 1770, which had virtually cornered the market by 1790. Carpet manufacturing was another branch of the woollen industry which flourished in Stirling, and in 1792 there were thirty to forty looms in the town, while in 1796 the price of Stirling's 'Scotch carpet' was from two to four shillings a yard. A century later, the Forthbank carpet works still existed. Cotton cloth was also being manufactured and the introduction of the Spinning Jennies in 1791 gave this a big boost; by 1836 it was the most important industry in the town. About 40 little girls were also employed in cotton embroidery. The Carron Iron Works had opened in 1759 and the development of a substantial coal industry at Plean and Bannockburn was well underway by 1800. This in turn led to an iron industry with four nail-making manufacturers in the town, which mostly employed little boys. Brewing, distilling and tanning were other important industries and, by the 1790s, papermaking was installed at Bridge of Allan. There was soap- and candle-making before the introduction of gas and electric lighting, lime-burning and brick-making. Coach-making was another traditional craft, and shipbuilding also was important, as the River Forth was tidal as far as Stirling, and this also supported rope-making. There were important continental links as a result. In 1836 Stirling was a busy port with exports to many parts of the world. Stirling Old Bridge was a 'gateway to the North'. All this contributed to an increase in population, exploited labour, and resulted in poor housing conditions. The one-roomed cottage was general in Lowland Scotland at the time.

Working conditions were harsh. Children from eight to 15 were employed in the factories. Little girls worked at the woollen mills from 6am to 8pm with a two-hour break for meals and they were paid 2s.9d. per week. Boys from the Edinburgh orphanages were employed at the nail-making businesses. They were bound to their masters for six years during which they worked for 14 hours a day. The youngest were six or seven years of age; they had food and lodging and were paid, but they wore only rags. However, many of the boys' ankles became deformed from long hours spent standing. Conditions for adults were hardly better. In one spinning mill, 140 adult hands worked six days of the week; during five of which they worked 11 hours and on Saturday nine, 52 weeks a year. Shops were open for 12 hours a day, six days a week. The mining industry was primitive, initially with pits, ladders and buckets lowered by a winch, but this gradually improved as more modern methods were developed with the opening of new and larger collieries. By the time of the 1861 census, the population had increased to 11,447 as a result of new industries, such as cotton coming into the area, and the expansion of the older ones. The pressure and problem of Stirling's growing population, as in many industrial towns of the time, was somewhat relieved by free emigration to Australia being advertised in the local paper; supposedly good wages were available there, at least for female domestic servants.

Methods of transport were revolutionised during the nineteenth century from horseback riding and coach travel to smooth and comfortable railways. From early in the century new turnpike roads were developing around the town and in 1833 the new bridge in Stirling, designed by Robert Stevenson, was officially opened. This greatly improved the road connections with Edinburgh and the coast. The macadamised, or hard-surfaced roads gradually replaced the mud from about 1815 onwards. In 1848 the first railway came to Stirling with connections to Edinburgh, Glasgow and Perth. Other lines soon followed and, in 1856, it was possible to travel from Edinburgh to London in from 10 to 13 hours. 1874 saw the town's first tramway system.

The downside of the building of the new railways was the influx of Irish navvies. The general problem of drunkenness was exacerbated. Poorer areas such as St Mary's Wynd became notorious for the number of its public houses. Overcrowding in the limited number of artisans' dwellings became even worse. Poor housing and the absence of elementary knowledge of hygiene, led to cholera epidemics. The first was in 1832, when at least 10,000 people were reckoned to have died in Scotland. Barrels of burning tar were set alight in the streets to purify the air. Tramps, vagrants and other undesirables were thrown out of the town. In Stirling there were 96 cases of cholera and 59 people died. Moreover, it soon became apparent that the infection struck at all levels of society and not only the poor. The cholera plague returned in 1848 and again in 1853, as it was not until 1841 that the link between cholera and contaminated water supplies was discovered. Streets in Stirling were then paved and guttered and general hygiene began to improve. Influenza, smallpox, scarlet fever, consumption, measles and whooping cough were also rife, particularly among the poor. In 1848 the first public waterworks was opened, and public health gradually began to improve. Stirling got its first gas lighting in 1826, and 1874 saw the town's first infirmary.

Political reform was very much an issue and the 1832 electoral Reform Act was seen as a first step. But the people of Stirling protested against the Corn Laws and the high price of bread, and a crowd of 1500 gathered outside the Corn Exchange to protest against the Government's policy when Cobden and Bright came to make speeches on the subject. The people could see for themselves the wretched condition of the Irish who came to the town seeking work. But it was not until 1846 that the Corn Laws were finally repealed and the high taxes on imported wheat and barley were reduced to a nominal sum. In turn this meant that the Irish landowners could no longer charge prohibitive prices for their corn.

Chartists too were active in Stirling and a motion was passed at a public meeting demanding votes for every man. This was sent to the local MP. Eventually, after many more battles, in 1867 every rate-paying male householder had a vote; this included many poorer households and increased the number of Stirling voters from 1272 to 4356. In the next general election these people chose a young liberal MP called Henry Campbell to represent them. He stood for land reform, universal suffrage, religious equality and national compulsory education. He eventually became Sir Henry Campbell-Bannerman, the Liberal Prime Minister, in 1906. These were exciting and 'interesting times' in which to grow up.

The provision of general education for the populace gradually increased over the century. There had been a school in the town since the 1150s, run first by the Church and, after the Reformation, by the town council. In 1783 this grammar school moved from a thatched hovel in to a new building at the foot of the Castle Esplanade, now the Castle Hotel, where it remained until 1854. It had a fine reputation, but this was lost during the first part of the nineteenth century with the appointment of Dr George Munro as Rector (Mair 1990, 227). He was a fine scholar, but a dreadful teacher, and matters became so bad that, in 1826, his assistant teacher left with many pupils to start a rival school known as the Classical and Mathematical Academy, which was opened at the Guildhall. However, in 1854 the foundation stone for a new grammar school was laid. In May 1856 four classrooms were ready and the school was partially opened for lessons at 7s.6d. a quarter, which only reasonably affluent people could afford. English and commercial subjects were taught together with modern languages and classics and 378 pupils were on the roll by 1863. The 1872 Education Act ensured that the school was properly regulated at last. In 1880 both girls and boys were admitted. But this was only for the privileged. A ragged industrial school for destitute children was founded in 1841, and, in 1856, it moved into new purpose-built premises; it depended on charity, the pupils were in rags, and two pigs were kept in the backyard. The Church of Scotland was traditionally responsible for schools, but, in 1872, this responsibility was secularised and regulated by the school boards. The Carron Iron Works in Falkirk also ran day and evening schools, and finally there were adventure schools, which were paid for by the wages of the workers and were of doubtful quality. The churches ran Sunday schools for the instruction of young men in reading. There were also small private educational establishments for young ladies. These provided 'vigilant superintendence' and classes in English, commercial education, Latin, French and German, piano and religious instruction.

Stirling is rightly proud of its School of Arts founded in 1825 as one of the earliest Mechanics' Institutes. These were 'to give the workman a knowledge of the scientific principles underlying his craft' and led to classes for more elementary instruction. The Institute had a good library and apparatus for experiments. There were also many cultural events, and the Stirling Natural History and Archaeological Society was founded in 1878 as the Stirling Field Club, which was also amongst the earliest of its kind.

In contrast to the development of the town's culture, many people were still living one family to a room in 1870. There were over 90 public houses and drunkenness was rife. Much of the work against drunkenness was undertaken by the churches, and in 1848, Mr Peter Drummond, a local seedsman, issued his first tract against the desecration of the Sabbath (Stirling Public Libraries 1909, 86) For some years Drummond had been troubled by the amount of drunkenness in the neighbouring village of Cambuskenneth, where large numbers of people resorted on Sundays during the fruit-picking period in the summer and autumn, spending the Lord's Day in idleness and drunkenness and pleasure. He tried talking to people to little effect and so the idea of the *Stirling Tract Enterprise* was born. This was a real success and became widely known. Drummond was an elder of the Free Church of Scotland and an evangelist. His *Tracts* spoke out strongly against drunkenness, as well as other evil practices such as fruit-picking on the Sabbath instead of church attendance.

Religion and the power of the church were very strong in Victorian Stirling. Theology was taken seriously, and differences between the fissiparous sects even led to the division of the Holy Rude Church by a wall, erected in the seventeenth century, so that those of different persuasions could worship seperately, in what were known as the East and West Churches. A main source of conflict was how far the state should be allowed to interfere in church matters, and some in Stirling disapproved of the Church of Scotland's increasingly moderate views. The Great Disruption of 1843 arose from the question as to who should appoint church ministers – the congregation, or the local 'heritors', who may well have built the church. Some 474 ministers believed so strongly that ordinary parishioners should have the final say that they broke away to form the Free Church of Scotland. In 1847 there were no less than seven different persuasions operating in Stirling: the Church of Scotland; the Free Church of Scotland; the Reformed Presbyterians; the Episcopalians; the Baptist Church; the Methodists; and the Congregationalists. And there was a Roman Catholic Church for the Irish immigrants.

This is the general background of the society in which Christian Maclagan lived from the age of around ten to the end of her long life; poverty, bad housing and drunkenness rife to the accompaniment of extremely fierce religious convictions, growing political awareness and a culturally conscious town.

2   Personal history and development of archaeological ideas

Christian Maclagan's life-span coincided almost exactly with that of her much-admired sovereign, Queen Victoria, to whom, by permission, she dedicated her first book. She must have felt that here at last, with a woman at the helm, there was a chance for greater recognition for women in society. Queen Victoria was born in 1819 and acceded to the throne in 1837 aged 18. In Stirling there were celebratory dinners and public rejoicing and five years later the young Queen made a tour of Scotland, arriving in Stirling on 13 September 1842. Christian must surely have taken part in the celebrations and, as a woman in her thirties, already well known for her philanthropic work, may even have been presented. There is an illustration of the Royal pair and dignitaries, outside the main castle gate (McCutcheon 1986).

Christian spent her earlier childhood in the country at Braehead Farm and at Underwood, near Denny, a small, new industrial town south of Stirling. Her father had died at an early age when she was nine, and shortly after this, probably in 1820, the family, consisting of herself, brothers and one sister, moved to Stirling and eventually moved to Pitt Terrace, a 'good' address. Christian was there in 1858 when her mother died. She was certainly predeceased by all her siblings and was possibly the eldest child. The 1861 census records her as still living there with two female servants.

Her family background on her father's side was of ministers of the Church of Scotland, one with strong Hanoverian leanings. They are described in the *DNB* entry as the Maclagans of Edinburgh. Christian would have known her paternal grandfather Frederick, a parish minister at Melrose, as he too died in 1818, only a few months after his son George, Christian's father. Frederick collected Gaelic poetry and attempted a Gaelic translation of the Bible as well as a Gaelic dictionary. Christian was engaged in writing a biography of him at the time of her death. There was thus a strong tradition of learning in the family, and she inherited her interest in Roman forts in Scotland from both her grandfather and father. Her father is described in one obituary as 'a distiller and chemist of good education', but there are suggestions that his early death was attributed to some scandal. He was certainly engaged in a lawsuit over the farm, which he rented at the time of his death.

Christian's mother was a Colville, a very respectable Stirling family with strong military and shipping connections. Janet Colville outlived her husband by 40 years and thus will have played the major role in the upbringing of the young family. It is highly probable that her Colville relatives helped her both financially and with careers for the Maclagan boys, of whom at least one died in Calcutta where he may have held some administrative post or been in the army. It was on the death of this brother that Christian inherited a substantial amount of money, which very probably derived from the Colville side of the family. And, when Christian herself died, she left the residue of her estate to her Colville cousin, Hugh Kerr Colville. He was known as Colonel Colville and owned a large house and estate at Bellaport, near Market Drayton, in Shropshire, where he is remembered to this day, as he did not die until 1936. A Captain Colville, his son, is recorded in the local church at Norton Hales as having been killed on active service in the 1914-18 war. With these connections, it seems very likely that Christian must at least have visited Bellaport and enjoyed the aristocratic surroundings and perhaps a library (see family tree, Appendix 1).

Few intimate details of Christian are recorded. The obituary in the *Stirling Observer*, comes nearest to bringing her to life in recalling the family's early days at Pitt Terrace, probably their first Stirling home:

> *Coming to Stirling from the neighbourhood of Denny, with her mother but recently widowed, and her young brothers and sister, Miss Maclagan quickly identified herself with the town of her adoption, along with her mother interested herself in charitable and philanthropic work in its midst. The household of these early days was a singularly happy one, the young people were all possessed of artistic and literary tastes which their mother fostered and encouraged, and all of them, received, for those days, a remarkably wide and liberal education. One who, as a girl, visited intimately at the Maclagan's said the charm of the whole family was indescribable. The entertainments were phenomenal and so different from any other house, so many interesting things were to be seen and so delightfully talked about, the sympathies of all the members of the family were so wide and their outlook on life and affairs so broad, it was a liberal education of the highest kind to be admitted to their circle.*

When her mother died in 1858 Christian was 49. She inherited a considerable fortune and used some of it to build a new house, 'Ravenscroft', in the newly developing Abercromby district of Stirling. She took a companion to live with her, a Miss Jessie Colvin,[1] who remained very close for the rest of their lives together. It was she who read Christian's notes at public meetings and accompanied her on her expeditions. Miss Colvin was an antiquarian in her own right and delivered her own papers at the Stirling Antiquarian Society meetings. There is possibly some confusion over the names Colvin and Colville. In one obituary (*Stirling Sentinel*) the residue of Christian's estate is left to a Hugh Colvin, a cousin, who was the chief mourner at her funeral and in another (*Stirling Observer*) it is Colville. The *Stirling Sentinel* also has a reference to a Major Colvin, another relative who was killed in the Sudan. Is this a simple confusion of similar names? Christian herself mentions a Captain Colville of the 74th Highlanders, who looked at the prehistoric temple on

Gozo on her behalf. There is some doubt as to whether or not the companion, Miss Colvin, was a relative of Christian's.

One important fact is recorded in the *DNB* entry (whose compiler had access to the lost autobiography). This states: 'Miss Maclagan was an artist of ability, although her right hand was rendered useless by a bone-disease and she could only employ her left hand'. Although there are several fine pen and ink and wash drawings of Christian's as well as sensitive pencil drawings and watercolours (eg **1**, **6**), this disability may well have accounted for the stiffness of some of the line drawings in her published works and may have made her feel at a disadvantage generally in public situations. Did she feel embarrassed because of this as it must have been noticeable, and was this why Miss Colvin was so indispensable and for standing in for her at public meetings?

There are a few hard and fast biographical details which can be gleaned from local newspapers and other sources. Years before her mother's death Christian established the first Mission Sunday School in Stirling. In 1844 and 1845 she is noted as a subscriber to the Subscription Library, and in 1866 she contributed £10 to the National Wallace Memorial appeal, as was only to be expected from such an ardent nationalist and patriot. In December 1866 she gave a treat for the mission schoolchildren when there was a Christmas tree, hymns, entertainments and presents of clothes. Curiously, in 1873, one year after its inception, she stood for election to the School Board as the only lady candidate, but later withdrew. Why was this? Was it because her arch-enemy Dr Beith of the Free North Church was also standing, and she feared his ridicule? Her involvement with the Church was thus nothing if not stormy. This passage from the obituary in the *Stirling Sentinel* gives the flavour of events:

> *A curious episode in Miss Maclagan's wonderful career was more ecclesiastical than antiquarian in its character. Following the late Rev. Dr. Beith out of the Established Church at the Disruption, Miss Maclagan became so enthusiastic in Church work that about 1865 she built a church in St. Mary's Wynd as a mission charge in connection with the Free North Church. Some years later she fell out with Dr. Beith over some trifling matter having no relation to the Church, and the quarrel resulted in Miss Maclagan resuming possession of Marykirk. Fully a quarter of a century ago the Free Presbytery of Stirling, in which Dr. Beith was regarded as a kind of Pope, had many a field day over Marykirk, one of the questions in dispute being whether the building, having been gifted by Miss Maclagan, was not the absolute and inalienable property of the Free North Church. Miss Maclagan, however, carried her point, and eventually handed Marykirk over to the Church of Scotland, and being afterwards endowed by the Baird Trust, it is now a 'quoad sacra' parish church, and the bad and bitter feeling caused by Miss Maclagan's erratic action has*

long died out. The congregation shut out from Marykirk took refuge in the Territorial School, and an iron church was afterwards erected for their accommodation. When this church was burned down one Sunday morning, the present United Free Church was erected on an adjoining site.

In 1843, after the Disruption, Christian left the Church of Scotland and joined the Free North Church, following in the wake of Dr Beith, whom she then admired. With some of her inherited money she had originally wanted to found a Mission Church in Calcutta in memory of the brother who had died there. When this proved impracticable she proposed to the Presbytery in 1865 that a Mission church should be built in Stirling. This was accepted and on 2 April 1868 the Marykirk, a simple gothic building, was opened. Sir James Young Simpson was present at the opening and spoke at the evening meeting.

Miss Maclagan has not only contributed the munificent donation of £1000 but given the site on which the church is built. Several gentlemen connected with the locality have also contributed to the erection of the church which is now clear of debt. (*Stirling Sentinel*, 14 May 1901)

However, relationships with Dr Beith eventually broke down for reasons that are not entirely clear and he became 'the arch-enemy'. In December 1875 Miss Maclagan brought a case in the Court of Session for repossession of the church and this was not contested. In 1876 the congregation left the church and the Marykirk was handed over to the Church of Scotland. The Free Church Presbytery heaved a sigh of relief:

Turning to the Marykirk, we may congratulate ourselves on getting rid of the unfortunate building ... It will be time enough to congratulate the Established Church on getting hold of it and its proprietrix when the terms upon which it has been handed over have been made public. (ibid)

Christian had hardly made herself popular by this episode, and perhaps the reason for her withdrawal from the School Board election in 1873 was connected with this as Dr Beith was also standing.

Yet there are many sides of this character to be explored. The loss of her brothers and sister must have been a very severe blow. Were they victims of cholera, scarlet fever, influenza, or diphtheria, which carried away so many young people? We are not told in the obituary. But we do know that a brother died in Calcutta, which was no uncommon fate in those days. Eventually her mother died and the greatest part of her life was spent without her immediate family.

But Miss Maclagan was not a woman to sit down and do nothing, nursing her grief. Years before, she had established and successfully carried on the first Mission Sunday School in Stirling, and her work in this and kindred directions was neither small nor intermittent.

Throughout her long life she was always keenly interested in social questions; for her the social conscience was no new development: but of later years the housing problem specially engaged her attention, and she had several schemes fully thought out which only increasing bodily infirmities of age prevented her putting to practical use. As it was, no scheme having for its object the betterment of the poor and destitute and hopeless appealed to her in vain and she did a great deal of truly charitable work which none but the recipients and those who were the channels of her bounty ever heard of. (ibid)

In the same obituary we learn that she was an ideal hostess to families and children in her garden and that, to those who knew her, the charm of her smile was not to be resisted. She is also credited with a sense of humour:

In the middle of a strong diatribe against some abuse (and one of her chief characteristics was absolute fearlessness in speaking her mind), she would suddenly see the humorous side of the question, and a sudden brilliant smile, and a gay laugh would come which quite transformed her, and gave a very human touch to her strong character. For she was a strong personality in every way, and while in the heat of controversy she could and did give pretty hard knocks without compunction, yet she had a marvellous power of attracting the affection and devotion of those who came into contact with her.

She always had a bright smile for children, and the charm of her smile and her strong sense of humour were appreciated by all. An ironic sense of humour comes out in all her books, and she could certainly see the amusing side of herself. She was capable of attracting strong personal affection and had many correspondents and warm friends. The *Stirling Observer* obituary concludes:

There is no one to take her place, no one who so unites the graciousness of the early nineteenth century with the strong vitality of the opening of the twentieth as she did. Indeed what always struck one with much force was her perennial youth. The questions of the day which are engaging public attention at the moment were to her as interesting as to the youngest, and yet she preserved a certain old world courtliness which nowadays is not produced.

Christian Maclagan's will, dated 25 February 1899, reveals some additional information about her private affairs, her friends and other associates. Despite generous gifts to charities during her lifetime she still managed to leave the substantial sum of £3,100.12*s*.3*d*. as her total assets. She had substantial holdings in shares and debentures in the New World. She left £1,000 to her cousin Major Hugh Kerr Colville, and a princely £600 to her maid Christina Turner, as well as £100 each to her two other maids. Other legacies ranging from £30 to £100 went to various reverend gentlemen and friends. The amount that remained after meeting these legacies she left (in a codicil dated 13 November 1899) to the Church of Scotland's Mission work in the Punjab, India, then under the care of Dr Hutchinson, particularly desiring that some of it should be used for 'all female improvement in domestic as well as in Christian knowledge'. Finally Christian willed that her bedroom and kitchen furniture, china dinner service and silver should be divided amongst her three servants. The total value of these personal items was £394.15*s*.6*d*. Her cousin, Major Hugh Kerr Colville of Bellaport, Market Drayton, Shropshire was her chief executor.

Educational and archaeological background

Christian received an excellent education for a girl, but nothing is known about its sources, except that none were institutional. However, she knew Latin, Greek, Gaelic and French and must have been reasonably fluent in Italian. None of this can have been owed to the Grammar School, which only admitted girls in 1880. It must be presumed that she was educated at home alongside her brothers. There were no significant publicly accessible libraries that she could have consulted in her childhood and youth. Even Macfarlane's Free Library was not established until 1855. Legislation governing the provision of public libraries came into force in 1853, but the local Public Library did not open until 1904. In any case, none of these would have offered the specialist resources she had obviously been tapping. Much later in life, as an elderly woman and a mature scholar, she speaks of a Rev Edward L Barnwell, of Melksham, far away in Wiltshire, who gave her free run of his library, and her second book *Chips from Old Stones* (hereafter *Chips*) is dedicated to him. As a woman she had no right of access to the library of the Society of Antiquaries of Scotland, but, being well off, she should have been able to stock her own library with the volumes she required for study. Throughout her writings there are references to many reverend gentlemen who assisted and accompanied her on her expeditions. She corresponded freely with them and quotes their opinions copiously; at least when they concurred with her own views. But all this was much later. Christian's father and grandfather, who were certainly very interested in Roman forts, probably had respectable personal collections of antiquarian literature, which she could have accessed in her youth.

Her frequent textual references to books reflect the breadth of her reading. She had read the *Agricola* of Tacitus, was familiar with Gordon's *Itinerarium Septentrionale* (1726) and quotes John Lesley, a sixteenth-century bishop of Ross. She had, of course, read the seventeenth-century works of John Aubrey and William Stukely. In her own century she knew Dr J Jamieson's *Vitrified forts of Scotland*; Dr Joseph Andrew's papers in *Archaeologia Scotica* and his works on brochs; Sir George Mackenzie of Coul's contributions to the same journal; William Chambers' work on the history of Peeblesshire (1864) and Pennant's tours; Arthur

Edmonston's *Notes on Zetland* and the works of George Petrie on Celtic crosses, and many more. She was, in effect, fully conversant with all the relevant literature on her subject. As for reading on foreign sites she quotes Rust's *Stones of Sinai* and De La Marmora on the Sardinian *nuraghi,* but failed, significantly, to mention the works of Giovanni Spano, which were important; even if she disagreed with him this would definitely not have prevented her from citing his findings. Perhaps this was one source she just missed. In the preface to *Hill Forts* she refers to Eddie Ochiltree's 'wallet' from Scott's *The Antiquary,* and to consulting scores of Statistical Accounts of parishes and many volumes of proceedings of learned societies. Clearly she did her homework to the best of her ability and with the resources available to her.

Dr John Stuart sometimes accompanied Christian to sites and, in his office as Secretary of the Society of Antiquaries of Scotland, he communicated some of Christian's papers to meetings of the Society. Perhaps even more significant was the clear admiration she attracted from the very eminent medical gentleman, Sir James Young Simpson. He was also a distinguished antiquarian and published two volumes of essays on archaeological subjects, including one on the mounds at Elephant Plains in Victoria, Australia. Simpson may have inspired her work and certainly spoke warmly of it at the opening of the new church in St Mary's Wynd, Stirling. The eminent Dr David Christison, who systematically published work on the hillforts of Scotland, refers extensively to her work, for instance in one paper describing the fort at Adifuir, although he reports that he found no evidence of her supposed 'covered way' (1906, 267) and he dismisses her claim that the fort was a broch (ibid, 269). She read Dean Monro's book on the crosses of Iona, the work of a Mr Row of Washington, USA, on 'cup markings', and works in Italian by Dr S Grigori and Professor Lanciani on Rome and Seville. In short, she was very well read and her books are peppered with quotations.

Development of archaeological ideas

While her background will have given her a reasonably sound base in archaeological fieldwork there is little to indicate how Christian arrived at some of the wild and sometimes quite eccentric theories which often colour her conclusions. To attempt to understand this, one must look at her strict Presbyterian/Calvinistic upbringing, which led her to believe in the literal truth of the Bible. The God of Abraham and Isaac, who would allow no false idols in His temples, is often quoted. Romantic theories about Druids and Druidisim were much in the air in the nineteenth century, but these were naturally anathema to her. She was also a devoted Scot, and Scottish Nationalism was in her blood. Therefore, when she encountered invaders, be they English or Roman, her blood was up. The Roman invaders were bad, firstly because they were pagans who worshipped false gods and graven idols and secondly because they threatened the pure, unaggressive natives who, although not Christians, at least did not worship idols since none were ever found on the sites they inhabited. These noble forefathers needed to defend themselves against the invaders, so they built many defended homesteads or broch towers of which they would have needed vast numbers all over the country. There were indeed many of them, but not enough to cover the country. Where, therefore, were the unrecognised remains of the rest? The answer was glaringly obvious to Christian: it was contained in the supposedly druidical stone circles. As druids and their 'so-called' religion did not and never had existed, then these circles must be the remains of the missing circular brochs in which the noble ancestors defended themselves. The apparently obvious impediment to this theory, that now only the uprights remained, was easily explained. For endless generations poor farmers had removed, by the cartload, the intermediate walling to construct their houses and field walls. As an archaeologist she should have accurately recorded what she saw, but interpretation was not frowned on so much in her day as it has been for succeeding generations. It is only fairly recently that we are again allowed to speculate via reconstruction drawings and the new medium of the computer. Yet is it not by 'sticking ones head out' that artefacts and other evidence are seen in a new light and are then open to reinterpretation?

It can be assumed that some of Christian Maclagan's travelling was done on the new railways, but much, especially to the remoter parts, will have been done by horse and carriage, presumably loaded with volumes for reference. She certainly travelled far and wide – to the Outer Hebrides and the islands of Islay and Canna and, apparently to Orkney or Shetland. She certainly went four times to the remote Mither Tap o' Bennachie in Aberdeenshire, no mean climb in itself. She writes vividly about her visit to Dun Tayvallich and other sites on the Knapdale peninsula opposite the isle of Jura, 'travellers coming here must bring food for man and beast as it is twenty-two miles from the nearest staging post'. And she was not averse to digging out muddy tombstones in order to record their carved surfaces or to climbing up high ladders to reach the top of very tall crosses. One incident she describes graphically took place on her visit to record the great cross-slab at Fowlis Wester at its site on the village green. After a ladder was procured for her to climb, the village schoolchildren assembled to gape and wonder at this extraordinary woman and her performance. She certainly saw the amusing side of the incident; her own account of it is quoted below (pp 98–9).

The constraints of the dress which was *de rigueur* for a respectable woman in the late-nineteenth century are easy to forget in these liberated days. A list of basic clothing necessary for the travelling woman written as late as 1911 is revealing (Steel and Gardiner 1911, 10). Underneath would come calico/wool or silk combinations or drawers (combinations were an undergarment, which covered the whole of the body with a flap at the back for convenience). Over that would come a bodice of stout calico and another lighter one of trimmed muslin. Stockings were attached to the bodice. On top of that the woman would wear at least three petticoats, one of which would be thick flannel for travelling. The crinoline was introduced in 1856 so, at least in the earlier days, Christian would have needed a petticoat stiffened or padded from the waist to knee length. Finally came the travelling dress divided into two parts at the waist. To finish off, a hat and stout boots buttoned up to the calf would have been essential. It is hard to imagine climbing ladders and narrow stairways or grovelling in the mud to lift fallen stones with all this gear and there can be no doubt that Christian did these things herself. Climbing to the top of the Mither Tap o' Bennachie in all those clothes must at least have kept her warm!

Christian Maclagan must have been inspired by her father and grandfather's interest in antiquities, but, she was only ten or eleven years old when they died in the same year, and we don't know when she started her serious antiquarian studies. In the preface to her hillforts book, she speaks of archaeology as being a science but sixty years old. Her first publication dates to 1870, when she wrote a paper about the antiquities of an area near her Stirling home, which was communicated to the Society of Antiquaries of Scotland and subsequently published (1871a). In 1870 she was already over 60 years of age and, as her major work on hillforts was published shortly after this in 1875, we can safely assume that her very considerable fieldwork was started at least 20 if not 30 years before that. She studied and made her 'rubbings' of Christian crosses and Pictish sculpture at the same time as her work on other monuments and the results of this work began to be made public in 1874, with a short contribution to *PSAS* on the sculptured caves at East Wemyss, Fife. Publications came regularly after that, both articles for the learned journals and four books. Her books were published in Edinburgh, three, presumably commercially, by Edmonston and Douglas (later David Douglas), and one, privately, by George Waterston.

While other antiquaries were travelling and recording Scottish monuments at this time and before, Christian seems to have been very determined and dedicated to the task, even conducting her own excavations. Her travels were not limited to this country as she went to Brittany and Sardinia at a time when bandits were fairly commonplace. As her book *Chips* was published in 1881, she presumably embarked on her foreign travels when most of her research on Scottish antiquities was complete. In 1881 she would have been 72 years of age.

The final question for us to ask, and learn from, is why did this woman blossom in the way she did? She certainly had the advantages of an early introduction to the study of antiquities and seemed to have had a stable and happy family life, despite, or perhaps because of the early death of her father. Then, before she was 50, she came into a considerable fortune. Many would think, even today, that now was the time to relax. Family commitments had been dutifully completed and the world was hers. She could have spent the rest of her life in good works, like her mother, and not exposed herself to the ridicule of both churchmen and antiquaries. But she knew well what she wanted to do and she did it. She used her inherited wealth to finance her research, which needed much travel at home and abroad, to publish her observations and views, to struggle for women's rights as she understood them in her professional context; but she also maintained her commitment to the poor of Stirling.

Up to the end of her life she was hoping that her 'rubbings' of carved stones would not just be a record, but would inspire a new generation of artists. How marvellous to be able to entertain such hopes for the future at the very end of her own life.

3 Development of archaeological work, working methods and publications

From an early age Christian had all the right background to develop her archaeological interests. She would have learned sketching and watercolour painting as a normal part of a young lady's education, but in her case there was a real talent in that direction – in one obituary she is spoken of as 'an artist of no mean ability'. The archive of her drawings and watercolours held at the NMRS in Edinburgh (D/44912 etc) has several examples of sensitive and skilled interpretations of ancient landscapes. In the earlier-nineteenth century this kind of talent in a lady usually led to her illustrating the work of male colleagues and no more. Margaret Stokes, of Dublin, who, undoubtedly, must have been an able archaeologist in her own right, made her reputation by editing, posthumously, the works of the Earl of Dunraven and George Petrie. Later she went on to publish books on travels in France and Italy where she pursued her interest in early Irish saints and the spread of Irish Christianity. There are parallels in these two lives as both started public archaeological lives at around the age of 50.

There is ample evidence in her written works that Christian knew all the leading archaeologists and antiquarians of the day and was well versed in their publications. The early railways of 1848 onwards, which connected Stirling with both Glasgow and Edinburgh must have been an enormous boon in this respect.

However, by the age of 50, her beliefs and convictions were firmly fixed and she was not averse to interpreting the evidence to fit her theories. She failed to appreciate the antiquity of the hill forts because she was obsessed with the idea that they were a form of broch built by the 'noble ancestors' as a defence against the Romans. Yet there is a certain mad logic in her thinking. Her unshakeable Christian beliefs, combined with Presbyterian convictions and her ingrained patriotism coloured and clouded her archaeological thought. To her the prehistoric Scots were not pagans, simply because no idols had ever been found in their dwellings. They were a brave, home-abiding people, who, when threatened by pagan Roman invaders, built their brochs, or defended homesteads, to protect themselves. She failed to appreciate the historical perspective in that many hillforts and brochs are much older than the period of Roman invasion, sometimes by several centuries.

At the anniversary meeting of the Society of Antiquaries of Scotland held on St Andrew's Day, 30 November 1869, the motion was unanimously resolved 'That a limited number of Ladies be admitted as Associates of the Society; at no time to exceed twenty-five in number; to be elected by the Council, and to be designated 'Lady Associates' (*PSAS* 8, 239). That Christian was only the second to be so honoured (in 1871) is a measure of the respect in which her work was held then. However, as a mere 'Lady Associate', her papers to that Society had to be presented by others, usually by the Secretary, Dr John Stuart, but, it seems very strange that this woman of forceful character and strong opinions, respected and loved in her own right, required the faithful Miss Colvin, and others to deliver her contributions at meetings of the Stirling Archaeological Society.

Christian's first major paper, 'On the round castles and ancient dwellings in the valley of the Forth, and its tributary the Teith' (1873a), must have been the result of many years of work in the vicinity of her home town of Stirling. Her descriptions of the locations of the various sites are innocent of anything as convenient as a simple map reference. Instead she chose to take the reader on trips up the Forth Valley (eg '7 miles further up the valley and on the north bank of the river; on the south side of the Ochil Hills' etc) and on that route we are informed about all the antiquities, be they cup-marks, stone circles or more recent carvings or constructions. Her style is episodic, as she lost no chance of expanding on the origins or derivations of place-names, or what old folk remembered of the state of the monuments in their childhood and the games they played. But what the style lacks in locational precision is made up for by her real appreciation of the scenery. Her's is the artist's eye, which comfortably incorporates both local legends and her own imagination.

She sets out her stall in the opening paragraph so that the reader can be in no doubt as to where her sympathies lie:

> *As the earliest historic notices of Scotland come to us from the pens of the Roman invaders, it may be that this fact has been the cause, though it is not a good reason, why our modern writers have so long and regularly turned their attention to everything Roman which can be traced in the land of Caledonia, and in their abounding zeal for that people, have wrongly given over to their credit many works to which they can justly lay no claim, and, at the same time, have passed over with most unjust neglect the remains which tell to us, their children, of how our 'crude forefathers', with noble resolve, withstood the military skill and prowess of the soldiers who had subdued the world.* (1873a, 29)

In other words our noble Scottish forefathers were much superior to the Romans in every way. This is a platform she adheres to throughout her writings without moderation, amelioration or deviation. Thus she sees the forts, brochs and duns of her chosen area as a first, second and third lines of defence erected north of the Antonine Wall by our noble ancestors to defend their own.

It was in this paper that Christian Maclagan first set out her major theory that all brochs/hillforts have a central tower and three defensive outer walls and they often had a covered defended entrance. Having developed this theory, all subsequent monuments of this type she recorded had to conform to it. The inflexibility of her mindset seems strange to us today when the frontiers of knowledge expand daily. Could this be a product of later nineteenth-century thought and confidence that they could understand and explain everything?

This first paper reveals the years of hard work and observation in her home area, and the intimate knowledge she had developed of it. This enabled her to take the major step of recognition that the fortifications which she described were not Roman, as she had been taught, but earlier in origin; that they dated from what we now call the Iron Age. She was certainly amongst the first to realise this; she had indeed become a pioneer of Iron Age archaeology in Scotland, yet she failed to appreciate how much earlier some of these forts and broch towers might be. Meanwhile she tries to stick to hard facts, but is unable to resist admiring and describing the scenery in a manner that brings the whole paper to life and is much more personal than other presentations. A modern reprint would make an admirable topographical introduction to the archaeology of the area; one could see her as an excellent guide-lecturer today.

In her next paper, on the subject of sculptured caves at East Wemyss, Fife, we are treated to a description of the caves on a hot midsummer's day when the village maidens assembled in the shade to milk the cows (1876, 107–8). For publication, Christian's drawings of the carvings (which were probably retouched rubbings) were deemed too large to reproduce, so earlier drawings made by J Young Simpson, which are poor by comparison, were substituted. But she did recognise the symbols as Pictish by associating some with those on the 'Drosten Stone' at St Vigeans in Angus. The date of this paper confirms that she was recording Pictish symbols and probably Christian crosses at the same time as hillforts and brochs, although her major publication on this subject did not appear until much later in 1898.

Christian's next short paper appeared in *PSAS* in 1880 and it was also communicated to the local Stirling antiquarian society. It was on the subject of two sculptured stones at Rhynie, Aberdeenshire, which she had exhumed herself after a builder had removed and partly destroyed them. This paper included two of her rare drawings of the stones (**54**).

Frequent papers also appeared from 1880 onwards in the *Transactions of the Stirling Natural History and Archaeological Society*, mainly on the subject of sculptured stones. However, there were no more papers in *PSAS*! Had she already made herself *persona non grata* in the higher echelons of the archaeological world by then?

A paper, again read by Miss Colvin to the Stirling society in 1890, was a first attempt at differentiating the sculptural styles of carved stones from east and west Scotland, which she enlarged on in her *Catalogue Raisonné*. She notes typically, that women are not portrayed unless they are sacerdotal. She also notes, with typical disapproval, that a sword was more frequent than a cross on the gravestones of men.

Is it to redress this balance that she had her own and her mother's gravestone carved as a cross in granite, and, in her case, laid down specific details for this in her will? She was not going to go unrecorded. How ironic, under the circumstances, that she was so soon forgotten.

One obituary notice laments Christian's 'inclination to see an Ancient British fortress in nearly every hill, a theory the truth of which is disputed by many antiquaries' (*Stirling Sentinel*, 14 May 1901). Her reputation was certainly tarnished by this over-enthusiasm for all things connected with the home-loving heroes of Scotland.

Christian Maclagan's first book and greatest publication was *Hill Forts* (1875). This vast and venerable tome was 'WITH LOVING AND MOST LOYAL HOMAGE/Dedicated by Permission/TO HER MOST GRACIOUS MAJESTY/QUEEN VICTORIA'. The book was probably inspired by the renowned doctor and antiquarian Sir James Young Simpson whose Presidential Address of 1860 to the Society of Antiquaries of Scotland she quotes in her preface:

> *"There are many departments of Scottish Antiquities urgently demanding, at the hands of the numerous zealous Antiquaries scattered over the country, full descriptions and accurate drawings of such vestiges of them as are still left. ... Scottish archaeology requires of its votaries as large and exhaustive a collection as possible, with accurate descriptions, and, when possible, with photographs and drawings of all the discoverable forms of each class."* (1875, half-title verso)

Simpson certainly respected and probably encouraged her. Others before her had published on various aspects of antiquities but few were so wide-ranging and exhaustive. Christian covers hillforts, duns, brochs, stone circles, crannogs, round towers and cup-and-ring-markings, all of which she deemed to be pre-Roman. There is an exhaustive gazetteer arranged by counties and detailing all known Scottish antiquities within her remit, most of which she had visited personally. There are 39 full-page plates reproducing about 120 original pen and ink drawings which were selected from many more unpublished ones. It is no dull catalogue, but is full of personal opinions and comments, folklore and even a recipe for Heather-crop ale. Her personality and sense of humour shine clearly through all her writing. We are also taken to Gozo, Malta, Sardinia, Brittany, Rome, Algeria and Australia in search of comparable monuments.

At first sight the book seems to be an undigested and disorderly illustrated compendium without any recognisable structure, but, given the perseverance to wade through all the various asides, topographical and personal anecdotes, a pattern does emerge. This work was written in a more leisurely age than ours when there was more time for such deviations which make it fascinating in some ways and frustrating in others.

The book itself is divided into three parts: Part 1 deals with general aspects of the monuments and here she sets out her main theories. The various categories; hillforts, brochs, stone circles, duns, round towers and crannogs are dealt with separately in that order. In Part 2 she discusses individual sites in detail. Part 3 comprises a gazetteer, an ordered list of antiquities arranged by counties, which, even today, is very informative.

The intrinsic value of this book is that it records, in detail, the monuments as they were seen in the third quarter of the nineteenth century, some of which are now lost forever.

In the preface, Christian describes herself as wandering over the country and then looking into books for further guidance. She found that:

> not even a "wallet" like Edie Ochiltree's would contain the ponderous volumes in which the needed information lay entombed ... in bulk and weight truly appalling to travelling humankind. Believing that, in pursuing their investigations among the early remains scattered over the country, others interested in Scottish antiquities would be glad to avoid the difficulties which I had encountered, it occurred to me that if the many extracts I had made from these ponderous volumes were gathered together, they might be rendered available for others.

One has visions of her travelling by horse and carriage together with all these weighty volumes to be consulted on site!

She stresses continually that she took all the measurements herself (with her umbrella as an unkind tradition still maintains!). Yet even David Christison, well respected in his time, who published a volume on hillforts in 1898, said he used his walking stick, approximately three feet long, for the smaller measurements. Christian also insists that she did all the drawings herself. Why did she not use photography which was available and was beginning to be used by some others? This was a pride in her own drawings and 'rubbings' which she says give a clearer representation than some photographs.[2]

But she was also arrogant; as she puts it clearly in her own inimitable style:

> while culling from the sources the records of facts, I have for the most part eschewed the theories founded upon them by the writers. Occasionally, however, this rule has been departed from, and I have quoted a few even of these, tempted by their amusing quaintness, or because they serve to mark the progress of Antiquarian knowledge and opinion.

How many of us do just the same thing today?

Christian Maclagan was a woman of firm convictions and these colour and influence all her work. The first, and perhaps the most significant of these, is her often stressed opinion that our ancient forefathers were men of courage and far superior to the Roman invaders. They were not a predatory folk but a home-abiding generation who were determined to defend their land; men of courage who sought to hold and keep their own. This was the reason why they built these strong defensive towers known as brochs and duns.

Indeed so strong were her views that she saw brochs in almost every round structure she came across in her extensive travels throughout Scotland, Brittany and Sardinia. To her, all prehistoric circular structures, be they what we now call hillforts, stone circles, crannogs or cairns; all were originally versions of the fortified homes of our noble, ancient and God-fearing ancestors. An ancient hereditary knowledge ultimately derived from biblical patriarchs such as a Job or Abraham enabled them to appreciate the inherent strength of circular structures. Thus, according to her theories, there must have been many hundreds, if not thousands more of these defensive homestead towers than those which we today define as brochs or duns. These views are what prompted the note in the *Stirling Sentinel* obituary. However, self-doubt could not have come easily to a woman whose investigations had been so personal, so thorough, so wide-ranging, and so laborious in an age without motor cars.

Hence also her repetitive attack upon Druidism related to the structures she studied. Such heathen idolatry would have been remote from what she maintained was the religion of 'our ancestors', who left no evidence of such practices in their dwellings. Moreover, she notes the prevalence of circular buildings, 'Older than Druidism – older than sun or serpent worship – old as the necessities of primeval man'.

In the preface to *Hill Forts* she says:

> *I had early received, with implicit faith, the theory by which the "Rings of Standing Stones", so thickly scattered over the country, were explained as the remains of "Druidical Temples," or at least connected with the rites of ancient worship. Personal inspection over a pretty wide field, however, elicited a series of structural facts which seemed quite irreconcilable with such an explanation. Thus I was constrained to look for some other reading of the megalithic puzzle; and, after long and careful examination, I have come to the belief that these upright stones in a circle had most probably constituted an important part of the uncemented structure of the dwellings or strongholds of our living ancestors, and were not their sepulchres – were not even temples of worshippers.*

The association of Druids with stone circles was well established in her day. These theories were first ventilated by antiquaries in the seventeenth century, such as John Aubrey, and were adopted by the traveller and antiquarian, William Stukeley in the eighteenth; more recently Stuart Piggott supported them, and they are still strongly held today (though hardly by serious scholars) and expressed in the form of summer solstice celebrations at Stonehenge and elsewhere. Christian Maclagan was thus at variance with contemporary received opinion both about the religious and the secular purposes of stone circles, broch and duns. On the basis of admittedly more thorough investigation, she simply knew better. For her the stone circles of which she found such ample evidence in Scotland were the remains of brochs, the fortified homes of our ancestors. This was abundantly clear to her and is set out clearly in many illustrations and reconstructions based on her theory.

Given her convictions, Christian then sets out in this book to systematically explain, and verify her views that all stone circles, cairns and hillforts were originally brochs or fortified homesteads.

Her next book, privately published in 1881, is *Chips From Old Stones*. It is short, and basically a travelogue of her trips abroad to Sardinia, Brittany and Rome. She made four summer trips in all to northern France to study the dolmens and stone rows, and one to Sardinia to study the *nuraghi* which she rightly thought closely resembled broch towers. There was possibly a visit to Minorca as she mentions the *talayots* and includes a sketch as an example (**42**).

Her third book, *"What Mean these Stones?"* (1894), was again on the subject of brochs. Although presented in rather a rambling style, it sets out a new idea. By this time she was convinced that the double walls of the broch towers were closed at the top. She had revisited Dun Carloway, on the Isle of Lewis, and the great towers of Glenelg in Inverness-shire and she was now convinced of her theory to such an extent that she made a papier-mâché model of the great broch of Mousa in Shetland in which the walls are closed (**44–5**).

Christian's last book was a *Catalogue Raisonné* (1898) of her 'rubbings' of Christian crosses, Pictish symbol stones and medieval monuments, which she had donated to the British Museum in 1895. These she arranged in '*schools*', with detailed descriptions of some of the stones. There is also a substantial section on the destruction of the monasteries in which the main villains are not the reforming Protestants but some of the local aristocracy.

These last three books are described in detail in later chapters.

Christian pioneered very detailed on-site investigations with personal recording and limited excavation. Her sketches were made on the spot but sometimes with preconceived ideas. This is particularly well illustrated by a sketch plan of the stone circle at Netherton Logie as she evidently reckoned it ideally should have been (**7**). Her attached notes suggest that she would like this to replace her original drawing which is not so regular!

In addition to their archaeological worth, her books are also delightful, informal travelogues which carry the reader from site to site through all the variations of attractive scenery. And if a local person had told her an interesting story, that is included as well. She often uses an apparently royal 'we' but it is not clear whether this refers just to herself or to herself and a retinue of clerical gentlemen and workmen. It conjures up a delightful image of two or three carriages filled with ladies and reverend gentlemen and a large travelling library, heading off along unmade roads in search of brochs or crannogs to the delight of the local populace. All in all, her books, if occasionally episodic and frustrating, make for fascinating reading.

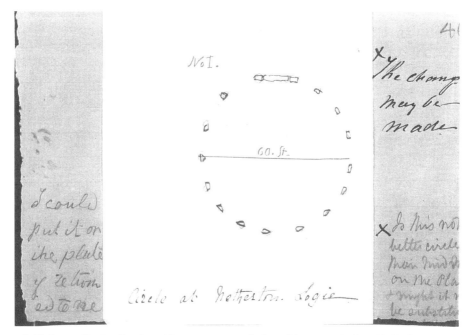

7 *Netherton Logie, Aberdeenshire: reconstructed plan of the stone circle – 'At Netherton is a circle of sixteen large stones, some of them 'in situ', some moved back and others fallen over. The long or lintel stone is 11 feet 6 inches in length. The circle stones, 6 feet high. All the lesser stones are removed.' (Crown Copyright RCAHMS)*

4   Four case studies

In this chapter four examples are set out in detail to try and give the true flavour of Christian Maclagan's style and the way in which she studied her sites. The first one is a breakdown of her first published paper, 'On the round castles and ancient dwellings in the valley of the Forth and its tributary the Teith' (1873a), with a sketch map appended to enable anyone not familiar with the area to understand what is meant (**8**). The second, taken from *Hill Forts*, is Christian's description of the monuments in the Crinan valley, Knapdale, Argyll, and again with a sketch-map (**19**), as this example is given to illustrate our author's typical manner of leading us through a landscape and appreciating both the scenery and the monuments. The third is her description of the Laws hillfort near Monifieth, Angus (previously Forfarshire), also taken from *Hill Forts.* The final example is a detailed study of her work on the great hillfort in Aberdeenshire, the Mither Tap o' Bennachie, which she visited on three or four occasions and where she conducted excavations. Accounts of this appear in *Hill Forts* and in *Chips.* In this instance a recent RCAHMS survey and my own observations on two visits have allowed me to assess and check the accuracy of some of her observations, at least where traces of the walls and buildings are still visible.

Other modern assessments of the various monuments can be found in Feachem (1977), Mackie (1975), RCAHMS (1985), Ritchie & Ritchie (1998). Details and OS grid references of the sites can be found in Appendix 2.

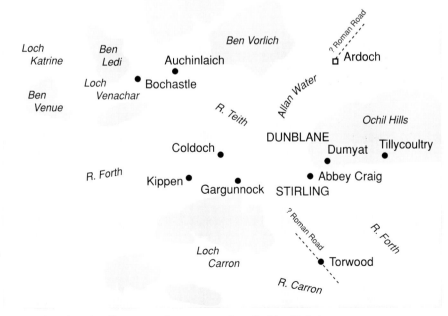

8 *Forth and Teith valleys: map showing sites described by Christian*

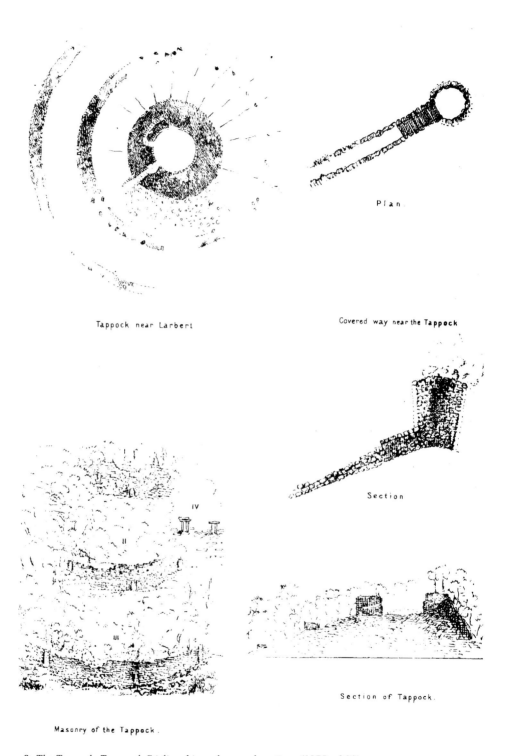

Tappock near Larbert

Covered way near the **Tappock**

Plan.

Section

Masonry of the Tappock.

Section of Tappock.

9 *The Tappock, Torwood, Stirlingshire: plans and sections (1875, pl 22)*

1   The 'round castles and ancient dwellings' in the Forth and Teith valleys

In the first of these case-study texts, Christian was thinking globally about the location of the various defended structures in her home area, and concluded that they represented a first, second and third line of defence against the Roman invaders. This means that she did not consider the relative antiquity of the hillforts, brochs or defended dwellings which she recorded, but it is evident that she was thinking about the strategic positions of the monuments and possible reasons for their locations.

   The first of these lines of defence which she noted follows the banks of the river Carron (Torwood, Tappock etc.); the second is south of the river Forth (Gargunnock, Kippen etc); the third line consists of Bochastle, on the slopes of Ben Ledi; Coldoch, Abbey Craig at Stirling and two forts on the southern slopes of the Ochil hills, Dunmyot and Tillicoultry.

First line of defence

The Tappock stands near the confluence of the Carron and Forth rivers (**9**). It is a strong defensive position overlooking both rivers and is now better known as Torwood (a broch). She stresses that it would have been surrounded by the great impenetrable forest of Torwood. The long, dark, covered way leading to the strong doorways of the castle would have given refuge and safety to a defeated army. She gives precise measurements and sees three defensive walls and a covered entrance. The hill was basaltic rock on which 'Murdoch, Duke of Albany, his two sons and his son-in-law, were beheaded in one day; and Scott, in 'Lady of the Lake' apostrophises it as 'Fatal mound, that oft hath heard the death-axe sound' (p34). Today three walls are confirmed but the covered way is disputed (Feachem 1977, 172).

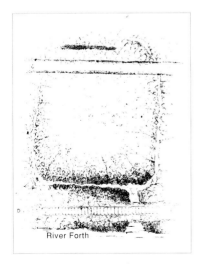

River Forth

10 *Kier of Gargunnock, Stirlingshire: plan (1875, pl 12)*

Second line of defence

This line follows the upper Forth valley. The first monument to be encountered is the Keir of Gargunnock (**10–11**), classified by Feachem as a defensive homestead (1977, 99), and here is a digression about place-names: 'keir' is obviously 'caer' or castle and 'knock' is knoll or hill, so castle hill. Again she finds three defensive walls although there are probably only two; but three fit her theory. The Peel of Gargunnock is down on the plain and here we have speculation about 'peel', 'pool', 'pol' and 'pow', all associated with water. This site could be what is referred to as '*Broch rems of*' on the OS map (NS 692 940).

11 *Kier of Gargunnock, Stirlingshire: view (PSAS 9, pl 1, detail)*

12 *Bochastle, Ben Ledi, Perthshire: section and plan (1875, pl 8[a/b] here amalgamated)*

As this site is practically surrounded by water, could it perhaps be found that all 'Peel' sites were once moated, she wonders?

Next up the valley comes the Keir of Kippen which had a circular wall 90 feet in diameter, which was almost 12 feet broad. In the vicinity were four stone circles and a tumulus. After these monuments the valley closes in so no further defences were necessary. Christian continues:

> *We shall now pass over to the north side, and there, right across the plain from Kippen is Benledi, and on its giant roots is the first of what might be termed the third line of defences to the north of the Roman Wall.* (1873, 36)

13 *Bochastle, Ben Ledi, Perthshire: the walls (1875, pl 7[a])*

Third line of defence

Bochastle Dun (**12–13**; Feachem 1977, 147) on the slopes of Ben Ledi Christian saw as having five defensive walls. and that the view from it was 'very noble. However

> *the once famous fortress is well-nigh forgotten, and so little indeed is it known that even the careful Burton, in his "History of Scotland," has called it a Roman fort. To see it is to know that it is OUR own.*
>
> *Sometimes, we hear regret expressed that on these buildings we find no inscription to tell the story of their builders; but are not the buildings themselves an inscription recording that they were no wandering hordes, but a sturdy people, saying, This land is ours, and we will hold it.* (1873, 37)

About four miles east of Bochastle was another fort at Auchinlaich but even then little remained except the levelling at the top of the hill which Christian recognised as the site of a former fort.

14 *Coldoch broch: interior (1875, pl 18[e])*

Next, in her consideration, is Coldoch[3] (**14**; Feachem 1977, 168) and why she did not see this as part of the second line of defence is not explained. Three or four years before she had mentioned it to J Y Simpson as it was then called a Roman well. She saw it as similar to the Tappock, thus a broch, and she compared it to the 'Pictish' brochs in Glenelg, Dun Troddan and Dun Telve, which she must have seen by this time (see below, cap 7). She also notes that the entrance was **closed from the inside** which she considered to be a distinctive feature of broch construction, also noted at Maeshowe (**39**). Again she gives exact measurements, and as a result of this the Stirling Archaeological Society conducted some excavations. Was she possibly the

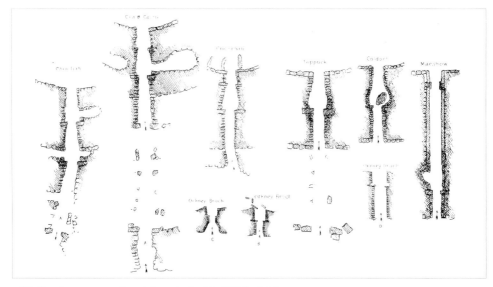

15 *Broch entrances closed from the inside (1875, pl 36)*

first to notice that this was a dun or broch and not a Roman fort? She notes six more probable duns in neighbourhood, as well as standing stones and cup-markings.

Christian considers that next in this line of defence is Abbey Craig (Feachem 1977, 157). This is a vitrified fort two miles east of Stirling which was largely destroyed by the building of the Wallace Monument (to which she had made a financial contribution ten years earlier).

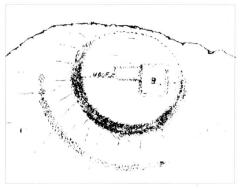

16 *Abbey Craig, Wallace's Camp, Stirling: plan (1875, pl 35[a])*

This is also known as the Wallace camp and hers could be the only plan recorded before the fort's destruction (**16**).

Dunmyot, or Dumyat, east of Abbey Craig on the Ochil Hills (**17**; Feachem 1977, 157; Ritchie & Ritchie, 95–6), is the next fort she mentions; it originally had three walls but it was much dilapidated

17 *Dunmyot, Ochil Hills: view*

for nothing is more common than to see the idler rolling its stones over the cliff, and then with eager delight watching their progress as they bound down the sides of the mighty precipice which surrounds this "castle in the air." (1873, 40)

Christian's observation of the three walls is vindicated by the RCHAMS plan of 1963 (no 68, 69–71). She also noticed nettles growing on stone heaps as evidence of disturbed ground and human habitation. This is now widely accepted, but she was an early observer of this phenomenon. Because of the 'pow', 'poo', 'pool' place-names, she imagined the British fleet moored below this fort!

Last in this line of defences is Tillicoultry 'Johnnie Mool's Hill' (**18**). Aged people in the village remembered playing there in their childhood when it had a roof of stone.

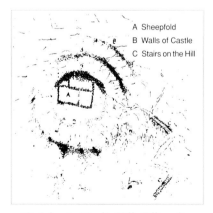

A Sheepfold
B Walls of Castle
C Stairs on the Hill

18 *Johnnie Mool's Hill, Tillicoultry, Clackmannan: plan (1875, pl 12[c])*

The view from the top of this castle was very fine; 'The wild, deep, rugged glen—the lofty mountain (2700 feet high)—the far-stretching valley—the glittering winding river—the distant sea,—all make up a scene of rarest beauty (ibid). This sense of enjoyment is lost in modern archaeological reports.

Tillicoultry naturally had the obligatory three walls needed for a proper broch, with the innermost thickest. Entrances were covered ways, although she does admit there was almost no proof, but the assumption fitted her theory. There is no mention of this site in the archaeological guides now.

There follows a completely irrelevant coda when she goes off at a tangent about an antiquity called 'Arthurs O'on'. Many people, she admits, have put forward interpretations of this odd name but her findings as 'a mere tyro' (novice) are based on 'facts not fantasy'. Oven or Aven is a stream; Ar is Thor; therefore the name means the stream of the river god. Tor also means most high, and she continues on these lines. All this is really nothing to do with the admirable main text but it allows her to finish on a very positive note. It also illustrates her habit, given the slightest opportunity, of flying off at what is to her, an interesting tangent. Arthur's O'on was, in reality, a Roman temple demolished in 1743, but recorded and drawn by Gordon in 1726 which Christian apparently was unaware of (RCAHMS 1963, no 126, 118).

I have gone into this first paper in some detail as it illustrates her style and opinions. Some of her main ideas are already clearly set out; the superiority of OUR OWN PEOPLE as opposed to the Romans; the three or more walls which she claims always surround these hillforts or brochs and the entrances which she claims were normally, or very often, covered ways. To these early ideas she sticks steadfastly throughout her work and goes out of her way to find them where they do not exist.

As a result of this paper she was elected a Lady Associate of the Society of Antiquaries of Scotland in 1871.

2   Monuments in the Crinan valley, Knapdale, Argyll (1875, pt 2, cap 2)

In the second case study we are taken on a visit to the Crinan valley and the surrounding area. The itinerary is somewhat hard to follow so a sketch map is included (**19**). She gives us a guided tour complete with appreciation and descriptions of the scenery and views, and includes her own observations as we are guided along.

Her first port of call is a group of cairns near Kilmartin where there is now a splendid visitor centre. These cairns had been examined by the Rev W Greenwell, of 'Yorkshire barrows' fame, who visited them in 1866, at which time he excavated one of them. In the midst of a heap of fallen stones he found the usual 'two concentric circles of upright stones', which go 'as we affirm' to the foundation of one broad circular wall surrounding a chamber. This naturally suggested a defended dwelling to Christian. In reality this is almost certainly the stone circle known as Temple Wood

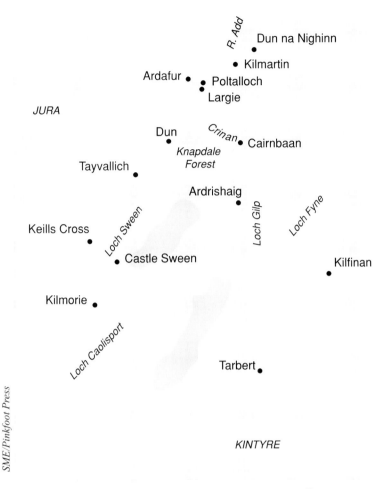

19 *Map of Knapdale, Loch Gilp and Loch Sween area, Argyll*

(Ritchie & Ritchie, 124). Then, in a rare moment of confession, she says, 'In a wood between this cairn and the farm of Largie there is a large circle of upright stones, the measurements of which we have lost'. Note the apparent use of the royal 'we'.

Next we are led to the circular cairn at Largie which is in the estate of Poltalloch which she visited in 1871. 'Our sketch' (**20**) is of the central chamber and she gives the dimensions;

> *about 23 feet in length, and 6 in breadth. Its height is 8 feet. This internal space is divided into four kist-like compartments of nearly equal size ... When the place was opened, bones and implements of human industry were found in it, also three arrow-heads, and many urns and fragments of urns.*[4] (1875, 40)

She then says that, while aspects of this structure 'suggest to our modern minds the idea of a sepulchre', the common Celtic tradition did not concur with this but

20 *Largie Cairn: interior (1875, pl 4[b])*

suggested they were places of storage. So her ideas of everything circular being a defended dwelling were not crystallised at this date and she was prepared to consider that it might have been a burial mound.

Now we are treated to some geological considerations. The River Add, small at Kilmartin, flows into the main Crinan valley. At no very recent time, she notes, the little valley of Kilmartin was a lake which was surrounded by tumuli. The Add was frequently flooded as is attested by a layer of blue clay which now lies under Crinan Moss. This clay layer is full of the remains of cockles and mussels which indicated that the sea must, at one time, have ebbed and flowed between the Atlantic and Loch Fyne. Now, in the Crinan valley, there are long lines of standing stones and could not these be the remains of tumuli as around Kilmartin; the intermediate stones of the extended tumuli having been washed away by constant flooding? Also there are cup-markings on one side only of these standing 'monoliths' which suggested to Christian that they were meant to be seen from one side only – the inside of dwellings, which is why they are so well preserved. This idea was developed later after her visits to Brittany (see cap 7). So here we have long lines of standing stones which were once parts of either sepulchres or dwellings. At Clava she thought the cup-markings were originally on the interiors of the dwellings (see cap 8). The logic may seem tortuous to us but Christian did attempt to interpret what she saw as well as recording it faithfully. She also noted that the cup-markings (**21**) were chipped by rounded stones and must therefore be earlier than the precisely carved Ogham inscriptions. 'On a seal of the earliest era, which was brought from Nineveh, now in the British Museum, we observed strikingly similar markings' (**22**). Note again the royal 'we'.

21 *Cairnbaan, Argyll: Cup-marked rockface (1875, pl 39)*

22 *Nineveh: Seals in the British Museum (1875, pl 38[a])*

In the midst of the archaeological survey she is anxious to display the beauty of the scenery and the historical interest of the area:

> *In a romantic glen near Ardrishaig there is an ancient hold called "the Robber's Den." It is small, and fully occupies the summit of a very steep and dangerous rock, on either side of which rushes and foams a mountain stream.* (1875, 41)

Next we are urged to visit (as Christian did in 1871) the Broch of Ardafur (Ardifuir, RCAHMS 1988, no 270). It lies on the Atlantic shore, north of the entrance to Loch Crinan: 85 feet in diameter; wall 10 feet wide and 12 feet high with

23 *Tayvallich, Argyll: two views of the fort (1875, pl 5)*

no trace of a staircase. There are signs of a second storey and a covered way to the entrance passage which extended inside. Euan Mackie (1975, 149) said that there was a stairway which Christian seems to have missed. Was this covered in debris in Christian Maclagan's time, or did she just not notice it? But she may have seen internal features which are not now visible . She compares it to Castle Coz, an ancient oppidum in Brittany where she had observed a similarly constructed covered way and door which served to strengthen the defences.

The next visit is to Dun-na-Hein (Dun na Nighinn, RCAHMS 1988, no 314).

> *This Dun is approached by going a mile or two north from Kilmartin by the road to Ford, but it is hid from the wayfarer by a multitude of surrounding hills, and when we draw near it we find that the one access is along a narrow ridge of rock, which connects the cliff on which the fort stands with its neighbouring mountains.* (1875, 42)

The fort was 50 feet in diameter and the wall 10 feet thick and there were the possible remains of a second wall further down the steep slope. A Mr Donald Jackson, the 'intelligent owner of the land', guided Christian and her party to this dun and answered her question 'How long did it take to grow 1 foot of peat?' He assured her that in that area it grew very fast, as an area where it was now four feet deep had grown within the lifetime of an old serving-man who remembered having dug down to the subsoil, so it must have grown some four feet in about sixty years. Christian had discussed the matter with several ministers in the West Highlands and one assured her that he had known drift peat to gather several feet deep in a corrie, and overspread the adjacent flat after a few autumn spates.

> *We mention these facts for more than one purpose, but chiefly as suggesting that it is erroneous to argue (as many do) that a superincumbent stratum of peat overlying "standing stones" or "Druid circles," as at Callernish and elsewhere, adds one feather's weight to the sum of their antiquity.* (1875, 43)

Tayvallich or Dun-a-Bheallich meaning the fort of the pass is in northern Knapdale where it guarded the pass leading from the bay of Carsaig to the bay of Tayvallich (**23**). But before describing the fort Christian is moved to extol the singularly lovely scenery and view of the Paps of Jura and of Loch Sween.

> *In trying to describe the shore, we feel we are speaking of "enchanted ground," so numerous are the lovely creeks along its banks, winding in and out among fairy woodlands, clothed with the richest wood, amongst which the stately rowan-trees, laden with brilliant berries, give a warm sunset glow to the woodland. The poet's description of the Trossachs may be fitly applied here:—*

> > *"Rocks upon rocks confusedly hurl'd*
> > *The fragments of an earlier world;"* (1875, 43)

The road down the eastern side of the loch from the Crinan valley had been newly made and seemed to Christian to be one of the best in the Highlands. It leads to Castle Sweyn (Sween), and she cannot help including a romantic sketch although, as she says, it is out of our period (**24**).[5]

24 *Castle Sween, Argyll (1875, pl 37)*

> *Some miles farther down the shore is Kilmorie Chapel, a lone and desolate place close by the sea-beach, holding up its lofty cross as if to hallow the wild waves of the Atlantic, as they break at its foot, and toss up those millions of mighty boulders … The dwellers by the shore told us of stones, more than a ton in weight, being flung aloft in the air, 10 feet upwards, as the Atlantic wave entered at the mouth of the loch.* (1875, 43)

It is here, Christian reminds her readers, that travellers must bring food for man and horse, as it is twenty miles to the nearest posting inn.

Back now to the fort at Tayvallich, which she assigns to a ruder age than Castle Sween. It fully occupied the top of the rock and was 69 feet in diameter, with second and third walls. She noted that the partition walls which divided the interior seemed to converge towards the centre. This is now recognised as the common 'wheel-house' construction which is sometimes found within broch towers. On a plain about a mile distant, Christian Maclagan saw, under the soft, deep turf, quite a crowd of circular buildings although only a few upright monoliths were visible. All their companions had gone to make lintels for cow byre doors and the like.

> *It is much to be desired that, when antiquaries see a stone standing alone, they would not take for granted that it has always so stood. We found living witnesses to the fact above related of this Argyleshire monolith, and in many other instances we have found that the stones did not originally stand alone, but were the remains of circles, and these circles again were the remains of broad circular walls—the walls, as we have tried to prove, of strong houses or forts.* (1875, 44 fn)

She concludes this travelogue by bidding her readers to 'go and see' this fairyland where they will find every kind of beautiful scenery, together with ancient remains of many different ages.

3   The Laws hillfort, Monifieth, Angus

The third example I have taken is Christian's study of the Laws hillfort (1875, 45–7; Ritchie 1998, 99). Here she visited a site which was already badly destroyed. It was estimated that 9600 cartloads of stone were removed from there during four winters from 1818. It is a rare example, for her, of using someone else's earlier material, plan and observations to which she adds her own. She herself noted the presence of small round stones from the beach, snail and oyster shells and one cowrie shell. There were still traces of pavements, vitrified masses of rock and 12–18 inches of black soil but there was not a lot to see in the way of features. However this did not deter Christian from producing a rather fine drawing of the base of a broch tower as, in her imagination, it might have been (**25**). For the rest she relies on reports and a paper written in 1826 by Jamieson who had conducted a survey and some excavations forty years previously. The plan she uses is taken from one made by a Mr J Salmond in 1859 and it is at once clear that it is not hers as it has a linear scale and a true north indicator. Christian herself never used such things. Her record is valuable however, because there has been no subsequent excavation and the site is even more degraded today.

The key, which she added to Salmond's plan (**26**), includes her own observations: This is Christian Maclagan reporting factually and well.

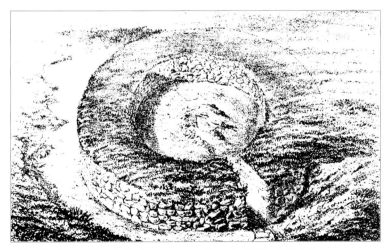

25 *The Laws, Monifieth, Angus: view of broch (1875, pl 29[c])*

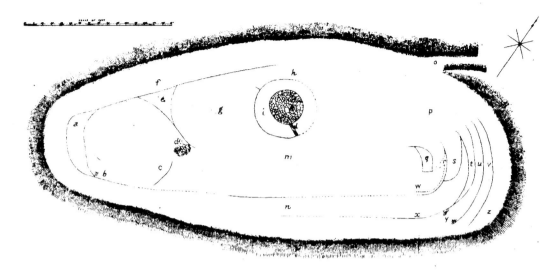

Ancient Walls, top of Laws Hill, Monifieth, Forfarshire.

a　enclosure showing great traces of fire, and filled with bones, shells, etc.

b　four rude steps. Foundation of wall here 8 feet below the ground.

c　a well-built wall, but has not been excavated to the foundaton.

d　portion of good flag pavement.

e　space, like *a*, with the wall all round facing the inside—bones, shells, etc.

f　wall, strongly backed with large stones.

g　not excavated. Highest natural surface of hill.

h　5 or 6 feet of burnt sandstone, mixed with charcoal.

i　rampart round the circle.

k　round floor, well paved with flag-stones.

l　paved entrance, with two projecting curb stones rising above 4 inches. On each side of one are wrought projecting stones, as if for a door, and on the floor to the inside, grooves were in circles, as if the markings of a door.

m　space, paved over with debris. Indications of the foundations of an older wall.

n　space between the retaining walls, filled with burnt sandstones.

o　apparent entrance.

q　walls not so well built as the others.

r　walls that have been rebuilt.

s　space filled with stones and earth.

t　west boundary wall built with flat stones.

u　space, with a faced wall of large stones on each side.

v　apparent outer rampart on the east.

w　filled in with burnt stones; charred barley found near here.

x　has not been excavated.

y　large boulder stones.

z　here the rubbish was thrown over when the hill was levelled, and the highest part of the walls on the east overthrown.

4 Mither Tap o' Bennachie

This section is based on my own personal observations in April 1981 and again in July 2000 in order to assess the accuracy or otherwise of Christian Maclagan's plans and observations. I selected for this purpose the great hill fort called the 'Mither Tap' in Aberdeenshire. This is because Christian visited the fort on at least three and probably four occasions, modified her views, conducted at least two excavations and recorded features which no longer exist. She worked under adverse conditions and with primitive equipment and, in the circumstances, it is remarkable that her first survey of 1875 differs so little from the latest one made only a few years ago. The mountain top is often shrouded in mist and it is usually windy and can be very wet. These conditions render accurate recording exceedingly difficult, as features come into view and then recede into the mist. The RCAHMS has recently (1996) made a new survey of this monument which makes an accurate comparison possible between Christian's survey and one done under modern conditions (**32**).

The fort is impressive as it rises to 1700 feet above the plain and it has been suggested by Professor St Joseph as a possible site for the battle of Mons Graupius on the basis of the discovery of a large marching camp at Logie Durno, a little to the north at NJ 699 275 (1978, 271–87). This battle was the final stand of the Britons against Agricola as described in Tacitus and it seems surprising that Christian did not pick this up or at least mention it, since, with her wide reading, she must have been aware of this source, and it would admirably fit in with her views on our noble ancestors resisting bravely to the last.

Christian tells us that Dr John Stuart said "the fort is yours", having walked over it without noticing the ruins, probably on a misty day! She is possibly the first person to have recorded it in detail.

She published two accounts of the fort (1875 and 1881), the latter being fuller and giving the results of her excavations. She notes that there are three summits or forts on the ridge of the Bennachie height. From east to west these are likely to be Watch Craig, Oxen Craig (the highest) and the Mither Tap with its possible west fort. A fourth fort is Maiden Castle, Pittodrie, in the valley. She must have had at least one clear day to have seen them all!

She records anecdotally that Sir Andrew Leslie, a turbulent baron of loose morals and famous for stealing ladies, occupied the topmost pinnacle of Bennachie which is almost 2,000 feet in height. This was probably Oxen Craig. In the earlier account, Christian notes only two forts on the summit ridge, an eastern and a western one, which she was a little unsure about as the natural granite fractured in such a way as to resemble walling. However, on closer examination she concluded that some was artificial and much had, as usual, been robbed away. These are the two forts of the Mither Tap itself. She published a convincing drawing which illustrates what she

27 *Mither Tap o'Bennachie, Aberdeenshire: view of fortress walls and entrance (1875, pl 1)*

28 *Mither Tap o'Bennachie: interior of second wall showing entrance and ruins of round-houses (1875, pl 2)*

29 *Bennachie: West fort (1875, pl 4[a])*

thought she saw, but one would have to make a visit on a relatively still day to ascertain the truth as far as it exists today at least. The drawing of the west fort (**29**) was done under great disadvantages:

> *for our party on this occasion ascended Benachie in an increasing mist, in the vain hope that it might be found a decreasing one. As none of the party had ever been on the mountain before, it remains a wonder to us how we ever found the* top, *but, with the help of a compass we succeeded, though our view never extended many yards beyond the circumference of the ancient fortress, and right glad we were even to see it through the cold drizzling mist which closed us in.* (1875, 38)

I assume that what she saw was a natural feature which only appeared briefly in an interval when the mist lifted. Christian herself seemed unsure about it.

The eastern fort is the Mither Tap and by far the largest. At the top

> *the rocky cliff is so narrow, one looks down on the wide expanse, as if from the "dizzy mast;" a wolf could scarcely have crept from one thicket to another unseen by the watchman aloft; and as its elevation is only 1400 feet, the distance lends enchantment without adding dimness to the view.* (1875, 32)

This is pure atmospheric imagination.[6]

The outer wall (A) she describes as encircling the entire fort as shown on figure **33**. The interior of this wall is shown as it sweeps round for 690 feet extending from the south-east cliff to the north-west one. It was 14 feet high in places and closely packed with the foundations of circular buildings (B). Also shown are the pathway (C) and round houses (B) inside this wall as it approaches the entrance (D). The southernmost house of the long street of houses inside the great wall was 30 feet in diameter with upright stones at intervals in the manner of the 'Druid Circles'. Is her imagination getting the better of her here and what she saw was a more recent structure? The entrance (D) was very wide until the workmen removed a great quantity of loose stones and found it to be about two and a half feet wide with three doorways or cross walls (**31** detail). She assumed that the present wide entrance was, of course, made for the carts removing the stones. The Reverend H Moir and his sons helped with this task of clearing the stones she faithfully records. The second wall (K) was represented by only sparse remains but the remnants of at least two houses were preserved within it (L).

Christian's published plan of 1875 (**31**) is very close to that produced by the RCAHMS survey (**32**) whereas her later one (1881, pl 6) (**33**) is not so accurate in shape but has more information on internal features. This seems strange as she presumably had the earlier map for reference and did not go to all the trouble of resurveying it. The second plan shows the overall shape as more rounded and with

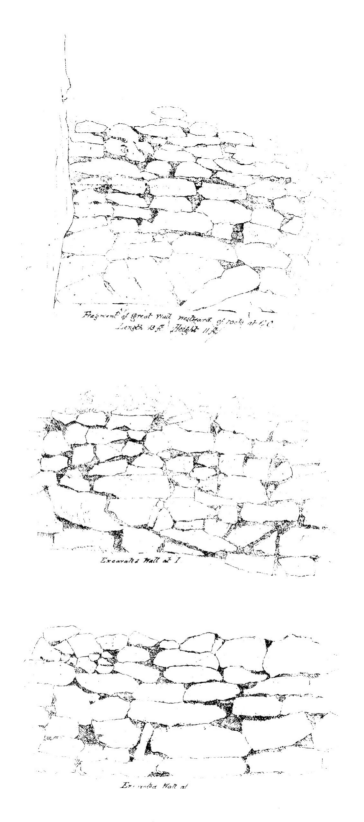

Fragment of Great Wall northward of rock at CC
Length 19 ft   Height 11 ft

Excavated Wall at I

Excavated Wall at

30 *Mither Tap o'Bennachie: excavated sections of great wall and west fort (1881, pl 7, details)*

three walls, more like a broch. Was her obsession with seeing 'brochs on every hilltop' getting the better of her previous interpretation? Certainly it is easy today to imagine hillforts situated on suitable looking hills where they do not exist in reality.

After 1875 she visited Bennachie on at least three further occasions. In 1876 she excavated at least 40 feet of the walls and a continuous row of circular houses; that is to say she directed workmen to do the actual digging as was normal in those days. In 1878 she made a thorough investigation with the help of employees of Mr Leslie of Fetterean and Balquhain. She found that a gallery and structures extended 600 feet inside the great or first wall. This wall was in a dangerous state, but both she and the workmen were satisfied that it did go all round the fort. They dug eight feet down by the external surface of the wall but dared go no further 'as both life and limb were in danger'.

A second wall (K) was traced for 400 feet and four round houses were now found inside it (L). There was a mass of debris, sometimes to a depth of 20 feet which they must have cleared in order to establish this fact. The entrance at the north west she now thought was not the original one and reckoned that stones had been carted from the entrance (D) as she found two 'bores' for gunpowder. She identified two more houses within the external enclosure. She now thought the true ancient entrance (P) was on the western side. It was, she thought, a covered way, 40 feet in length with walls still three feet high. She identified a possible third wall near the summit (M). In 1879, at the age of seventy, she paid her last visit to the fort.

This survey and excavation would seem to be a case of good and probably fairly accurate recording for the time. It certainly has evidence of much that has disappeared over the last hundred years, but also includes a group of round houses where it seems most unlikely that they could ever have existed.

The site is undated, but its use of precipitous rocky outcrops might suggest a Dark Age Pictish date on analogy with others discussed by Feachem and others (1955).

She ends, typically with an interesting digression on the word 'maid' as in Maiden Castle at Pittodrie. She suggests that it is derived from the verb 'to make' as it was still used by country folk, 'an ill maiden road'. Thus Maeshowe and Maiden Causeway simply mean a made structure of some kind. I have no idea if this interpretation stands up, but it is an interesting one.

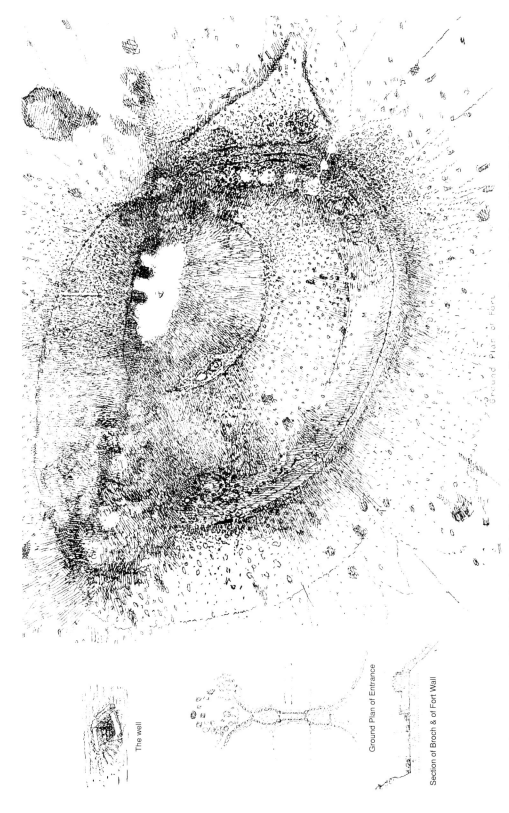

The well

Ground Plan of Entrance

Section of Broch & of Fort Wall

31 *Mither Tap o' Bennachie: plan of the fort, with details – plans of entrance and well, and section of broch and fort wall (1875, pl 3).*

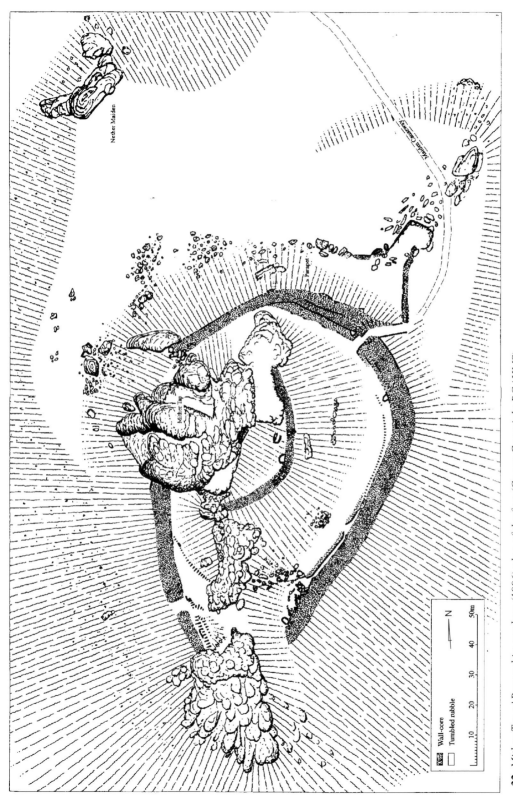

32 *Mither Tap o' Bennachie: modern (1996) plan of the fort (Crown Copyright RCAHMS)*

Plate VI

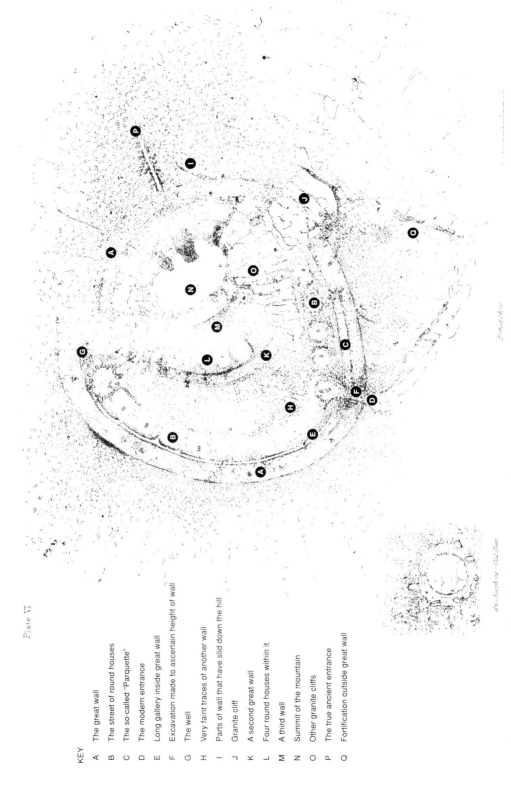

KEY

A   The great wall
B   The street of round houses
C   The so-called "Parquette"
D   The modern entrance
E   Long gallery inside great wall
F   Excavation made to ascertain height of wall
G   The well
H   Very faint traces of another wall
I   Parts of wall that have slid down the hill
J   Granite cliff
K   A second great wall
L   Four round houses within it
M   A third wall
N   Summit of the mountain
O   Other granite cliffs
P   The true ancient entrance
Q   Fortification outside great wall

33   *Mither Tap o'Bennachie: plan of the fort (1881, pl 6 – with modern labelling superimposed)*

5   Strange conclusions – Christian Maclagan's views on brochs

I invite my readers to suspend all their current beliefs about brochs and to approach the subject with a completely open mind, to imagine themselves back in the middle of the nineteenth century when little research had been done in this field. My subject looked at what she saw on the ground with meticulous care and drew her own conclusions! She was very thorough in her investigations and visited personally at least 70 or more sites, some several times, no mean feat in itself when transport was not as convenient as it is today.

Christian Maclagan's main views have already been explained in Chapter 2. Her platform is that all prehistoric round structures are the remains of the defensive homesteads of the Scottish ancestors (today, some at least, are referred to as Atlantic Round Houses; see Armit 1990, 16)

In the Preface to *Hill Forts* she says

> *I had early received, with implicit faith, the theory by which the "Rings of Standing Stones," so thickly scattered over the country, were explained as the remains of "Druidical Temples;" or, at least, as connected with the rites of ancient worship. Personal inspection over a pretty wide field, however, elicited a series of structural facts which seemed quite irreconcileable with such an explanation. Thus I was constrained to look for some other reading of the megalithic puzzle; and, after long and careful examination, I have come to the belief that these upright stones in circle had most probably constituted an important part of the uncemented structure of the dwellings or strongholds of our living ancestors, and were not their sepulchres— were not even temples of worshippers.*

Hill Forts is the source of most of the following information and all the illustrations are her own work and drawn at the sites themselves.

What then were these stone circles of which she found such ample evidence in Scotland?

Stone circles are denuded brochs

Christian Maclagan had a practical turn of mind and she set it to work out how these broch towers had originally been built. As they were built without mortar they surely needed perpendicular uprights to support the structures. And what could better provide this than the remaining uprights of 'so-called' druidical stone circles? She had seen with her own eyes evidence of the destruction caused by farmers removing

S W

Section, Restored Wall at A

Restoration - Auquorthies.

Birds eye View of Auquorthies Circle

S W Stone Auquorthies Circle

Restoration of Auquorthies

A

34 *Stone circle seen as a broch: Easter Aquorthies, Aberdeenshire (1875, pls 27 & 28, details)*

cartloads of stones from prehistoric stone structures, as at the ancient fortification at Monifieth Laws.

An interesting glimpse into Christian's working methods is provided by an unpublished sketch of a circle at Netherton Logie (**7**). She started with the conviction that all stone circles were symmetrical and drew a pencil circle with a compass. Presumably she fitted existing stones in first. The absent stones were then fitted into this perfect circle. She suggests to her publisher that this drawing should replace the original, sketched at the site, which was not so regular (see plan of Kercode where this system is used, **48**).

Initially her views are perhaps best explained with regard to the recumbent stone circle at Easter Aquorthies (**34**). This has not been excavated, as has the now better known one at Loanhead of Daviot. She initially gives a 'bird's eye' view of Aquorthies showing perhaps 11 still-standing stones of which there are today only nine. The north indicator, which she never routinely used, is eccentrically placed and skewed to show the recumbent stone/lintel at the top. Next she illustrates the recumbent stone (or fallen lintel) with the two fallen supposed supports which is followed by a reconstruction according to her theory. The theory is that the lintel or entrance stone was initially supported by two low upright stones which, in this case, have fallen inwards. The restoration drawing shows how they originally functioned. In examples where these low upright stones no longer exist Christian's explanation is that no stones of suitable height were available at the time of building and that there were originally piers or pillars of smaller stones constructed to perform a similar function. These, of course, have been removed typically by the farmer with his cart. The lintels (recumbent) stones are massive and could not possibly have been supported by the large upright stones alone. The large size of the lintel stones is accounted for by the weight of the large superstructure which, in her view, they had to carry. The tall pillar stones at each side of the recumbent stones are necessary to check and solidify the structure. For instance, in no way could the lintel have stood on the top of the two supporting stones at the similar circle at Dyce (**35**), which neatly proves her point. Her restoration drawing of the Aquorthies 'Broch' and section of the wall at 'A' completes the

35 *Plan and sections of Dyce stone circle (1875, pl 28, detail)*

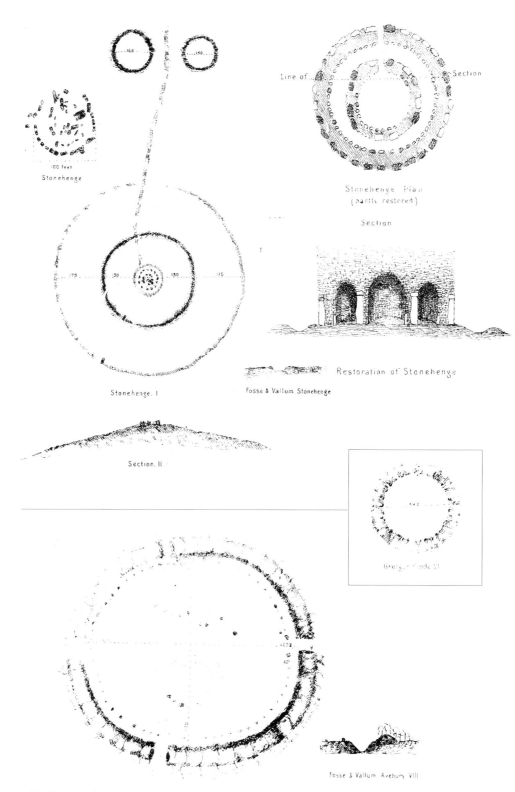

36 *Stone circles seen as brochs: Stonehenge; Avebury; Ring of Brodgar (inset) (1875, pls 14 & 15, details)*

story. At Dyce, Christian certainly noticed the central cairn, now known to be so typical of all these monuments, but she failed to realise what it was.

A second firm conviction of Christian's was that the foundations of the standing stones are not deep but are only notched into the ground where this is not level. To her this sketchy foundation proves, unaccountably, that the uprights were there to give stability to the intervening walls which have been robbed over time. Indeed, to add strength to her theory, a relative, Captain Colville of the 74th Highlanders, had examined the temple on Gozo on her behalf and noted evidence of upright pillars used as binding stones. Yet she fails to explain why so many of the great stones still stand upright when the walls have gone and does not ever seem to have actually attempted to excavate around any standing stone. Her theory was enough to substantiate this point together with the evidence of her eyes. She clearly did not know about Arbour Low in Derbyshire where all the uprights have been thrown (or fallen) down or she would have had a field day there!

This theory is developed to its ultimate conclusions with Christian's typical thoroughness until Stonehenge, Avebury, and even the great Ring of Brodgar, become elements of fortified dwellings. The plans and restoration drawings of Stonehenge well illustrate the theory and her consequent assumptions. Her plan, section and subsequent assumed restoration drawings illustrate the point (**36**).

> *The outermost circle represents a trench, which appeared to be as real a part of the great whole as the second. The innermost of the three circles is more doubtful, but allowing for the many disturbing influences, there still remain traces of its former existence. The fact of the stones forming an ellipse within the great circle, and placed nearer to one side of it than the other, is a feature noticeable in many Scotch circles. The nearness is towards that part of the circle where the door has been, or still is; and Stonehenge has been arranged for one of the narrow doorways (2^1/$_2$ feet) of these days, for a line passes through both circle and ellipse at that point. Again circles of small stones within circles of large ones, as at Stonehenge, is quite a common feature in the north, where they form the surface line or elevation of the two sides of one wall. We assume of course that in a climate like ours these buildings were all covered by a roof.*
> (p70)

Here we clearly have a large hilltop broch with an inner tower, a main entrance through the outer tower and two subsidiary ones through the inner tower. The fallen stones are the result of shallow foundations so that they collapsed once the intervening walls had been removed.

Avebury is a little more difficult to adapt but with the right amount of determination it can be seen as an exceptionally deep-ditched defended circular enclosure with two towers inside it constituting the dwelling places. The ring of

Brodgar can be similarly interpreted (**36** inset), as can the stones of Stenness. Silbury Hill is seen as an exceptionally large broch.

Moreover, Christian is ready to make short work of the wild theories of others in the field before her. Where would be the **clear evidence** John Aubrey had claimed to possess that both Stonehenge and Avebury were **Druid Circles**? Others had been even more specific:

> *Twining calls Avebury a temple of Terminus, whilst the Rev. J. B. Deans thinks it was used for serpent-worship. Sir Christopher Wren believed the great "Sarsen stones" on Salisbury Plain were cast up by a volcano. Stukeley thought that "when the chalky soil of these plains hardened, it spewed out the most solid body of the stones." Such were the conclusions of the wise men of their day.* (p71)

Compared with such nonsense, her suggestions were eminently sensible.

Cairns as Brochs

To the south-west of Inverness, at Clava, near the Culloden battlefield, there is a group of three cairns, each surrounded by a stone circle; two are passage graves and one a ring cairn with no entrance. Christian saw nine, and possibly up to thirteen circles of standing stones all of which she interpreted as the remains of brochs. Number VI on her plan (**37**) has a central chamber, 12 feet in diameter, surrounded by a circular

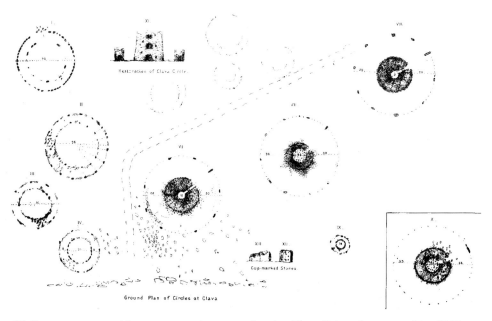

37 *Passage graves and barrow cemeteries seen as brochs: Clava Cairns, Inverness-shire (1875, pl 26)*

wall, 18 feet broad, carefully and well-built of stone throughout. She thought the builders first laid out on the level ground two circular rows of large heavy stones for the foundation of the future walls. Either these stones were large enough to keep their position by the force of their own dead-weight or the ends of the taller and slighter ones were sunk into the ground to act as binding stones for the superimposed structure. The 'ponderous' wall was then reared, the stones becoming smaller with each succeeding layer and the masonry gradually inclined inwards until the diameter was lessened by two feet. The height of the chamber was apparently about 10 feet at the time and she thought that it would have continued to narrow until the top was closed. Above the main chamber there may have been another one of the same size as the strength of the wall would have been sufficient to bear it. There was an entrance through the great wall two feet wide, 'doubtless' originally roofed with large slabs which reached from side to side. Thus we have a broch or fortified dwelling tower which is surrounded by a ring of standing stones. It would be fascinating to know how much of this supposed structure really existed at the time when Christian saw

38 *Barrow cemetery seen as a group of brochs: Clava Cairns, Inverness-shire (1875, pl 25)*

it but, sadly, only an indistinct pile of stones in an artistic setting (**38**) actually appears in her illustration.

Number VII on Christian's drawing is, in fact, a ring cairn. She says it is normally noticed as a mere heap of stones, but its central chamber was 22 feet in diameter and the wall 17 feet in breadth. Christian got a little over-enthusiastic here and inserted an entrance which can never have been there. Number VIII is another passage grave.

Thus this extensive Bronze Age burial-ground is interpreted as a former city for the living, for as Christian saw it, people needed to defend themselves when they were still alive and had no need for what she interpreted as elaborate defences when they were dead:

> It is long since the dwellings of this valley were broken up and desolated, and they have been so much used as stone quarries that scarcely any debris is left, though the circles themselves are distinctly traceable on the ground. So

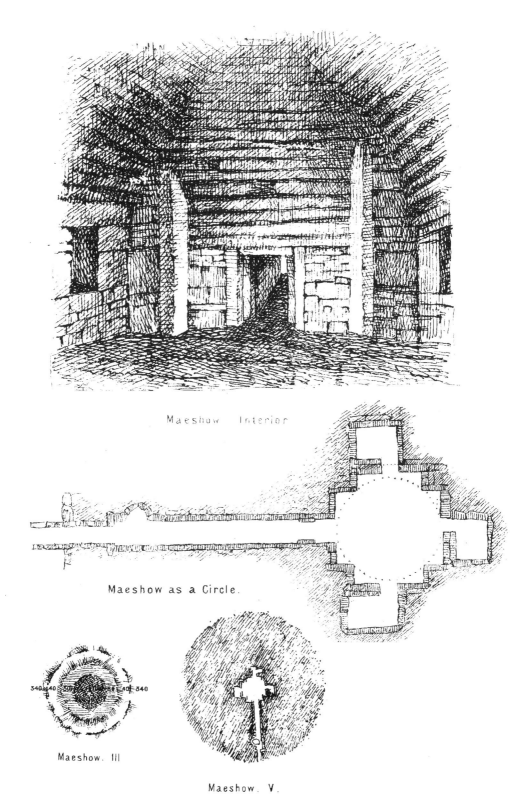

Maeshow Interior

Maeshow as a Circle.

340 340 340 340 340 340

Maeshow. III

Maeshow. V.

39 *Maeshowe as a broch (1875, pls 24 & 25, details)*

40 *View of Maeshowe (1875, pl 13)*

numerous are they that those given on Plate XXVI. are only a part of the crowd that has covered the whole area of this once thickly-inhabited "Haugh," but they are the most distinct in outline. In the adjacent corn fields are great stones, and indications of extensive circles, so that here has evidently stood a mighty city – not of the dead but of the living. (pp74–5)

The illustrations to all this are somewhat confusing because of her eccentric habit, mentioned earlier, of placing the north wherever it best suited her. The cup-marked stones on the site are supposed, naturally, to be the interior walls of the defended dwellings.

Even Maeshowe, the great chamber tomb in Orkney (**39-40**) is seen as a defended homestead and its development from a simple dwelling to a more elaborate one is demonstrated. The main evidence for the defended homestead theory is that the entrance is supposedly designed to be closed from the inside and the long narrow entrance tunnel was thought to be for ventilation (**39**). The main entrance, as seen from the inside, is typical of her eccentric reconstructed entrances of the recumbent stone circle 'brochs' with its large uprights and lower lintel stone. The height of the mound indicates to Christian that there may well have been a second floor above the main chamber as the structure could well have supported the weight! This upper room would have needed a window such as is found in the Sardinian *nuraghi*. The massive walling and immensely strong corbelled roof of the Temple of Haigar Kem (*sic*) on the island of Malta are cited as another example of a structure which must have had an upper storey, although there is no evidence for this. She had not seen it herself but had heard of it from a sympathetic relative.

Hillforts as brochs

White Caterthun is a hillfort in Angus which stands on a pronounced eminence. It is an oval fort measuring above 500 by 220 feet with what is possibly the most imposing ruined wall in Britain which may have originally been as much as 40ft thick. Close outside is a pile of boulders representing another wall about 20 feet thick. The combined tumble now spreads over about 100 feet and there are traces of two or more ramparts further out. To Christian, this is undoubtedly a broch of large proportions with an inner wall 25 to 30ft thick. As standing brochs with walls no more than 12 feet thick were built to a height of 30 to 40 feet, she assumes that this must have been at least as high. Outside this she saw the remains of two heaps of stones which would have formed the sides of one outer wall (**41**). Christian did not have the

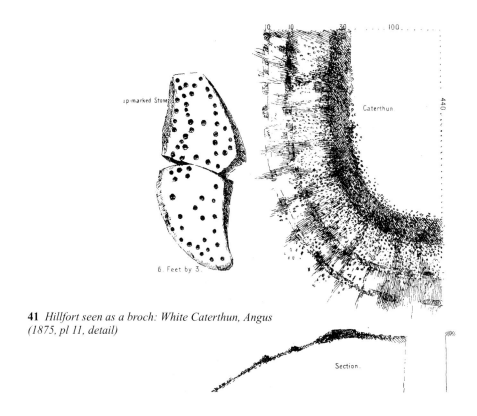

41 *Hillfort seen as a broch: White Caterthun, Angus (1875, pl 11, detail)*

advantage of aerial photographs to locate the other ramparts but she did notice a large cup-and-ring-marked stone (Ritchie 1998, 94); as she had noted that this was similar to cup-marked stones at Clava, her view was that these two groups of structures could be of the same date.

The Laws fort has an internal broch (see cap 4; Ritchie & Ritchie, 99), and here Christian also compares the broch remains with those at Clava (passage grave/cairns) and her drawings show closely similar features, which, to her, proves the point that brochs with massive walls are chronologically early. She sees distinct affinities between sites such as Clava and the Laws as both have several defended dwellings surrounded by defensive walls. And so she continues until nearly all the hillforts she visited are really brochs; and she visited and measured upwards of 40 of them.

Brochs – development of structural forms.

Christian gradually evolved a theory about the chronological development of broch towers based on their structures. This is imaginative and innovative but has many flaws.

Torwood Iron Age fort and broch, the Tappock (Feachem 1977, 54), Christian sees as the earliest form of broch structure because of its apparently massive walls (**9**). It is now regarded as an Iron Age fort with an early Pictish broch, pre-AD140, built as a defence against the second period of Roman occupation. The broch is built partly on the ruin of the inner rampart of the earlier Iron Age fort and partly within the interior.

Christian categorised the Tappock as an early version of the broch tower. It was a very substantial circular tower with an interior diameter of 33 feet with a wall rising to 18 feet or more, but she considered it had evidently been much higher than it was when she visited. The diameter of the wall increased at 8 feet on a line with the lintels of two doorways and provided the scarcements for the upper story of this building 'as all the evidence points to this conclusion' she says. The circular bend in the stairway indicates an upper storey, as the bend does not point outwards but inwards. The entrance passage at ground level was 23 feet long and extended beyond the exterior of the wall. It was roofed with great stones which extended across its breadth. Around the outer sides of the walls, upright stones 4 feet high and 2 feet broad, were inserted at regular intervals to strengthen and bind the masonry. At a distance of 30 feet from the innermost wall occurred another semicircular wall and again another substantial wall after a further 30 feet; the three surrounding walls again. Thus she saw a solid central tower with no trace of chambers but a stairway which indicated at least another storey with possible mural chambers. The entrance way led in a straight line through the three presumed outer walls. These external walls she saw as a simple way of increasing defended living accommodation if and when it was needed. This then is her definition of an early form of the broch as it has massive walls indicating original great height, an intramural staircase, for access to the top and three outer walls for extra protected accommodation. It has a covered, protected entrance way which reaches to the outermost wall.

So it follows that if the Tappock is an early form of the broch structure, then Mousa, in Shetland (**42**) must be a later development. Mousa has thinner tower walls and was incapable of a long life because of this slenderness (yet it still stands to 40 feet

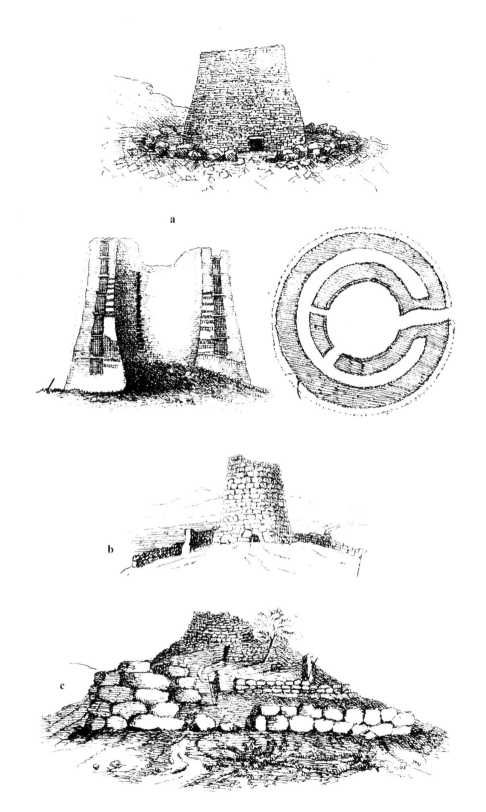

42 *Later broch: Mousa, Shetland (**a**) compared with Sardinian* nuraghe *(**b**) and Minorcan* talayot *(**c**) (1875, pl 17, details)*

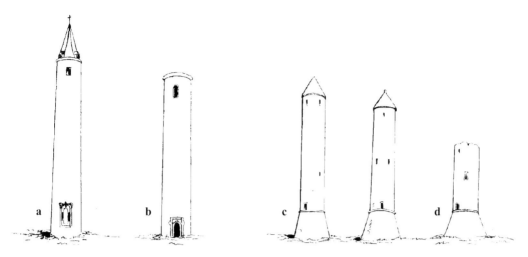

43 *Outline elevations of medieval round towers:* **a** *Brechin, Angus;* **b** *Abernethy, Perthshire;* **c** *Ireland;* **d** *Brunless Castle, Wales (1875, pl 39, detail)*

today!). In the chronologically later versions of the broch the walls narrowed and had cavities with a winding stairway and internal windows for ventilation. She pointed out that there was no need for external windows as the towers were for defence, and warmth was more important than light. The roofs were 'not lower than those of a "three-decker" of our own fleet, and "Jack" has no more light between decks than his landsmen forefathers had in these castles'.

She continues the argument logically by seeing the continuation of the tradition into medieval round towers such as Launceston, Abernethy, Brechin and Irish round towers (**43**) which have doors above ground level and no windows. Parallels are also drawn with the *nuraghi* towers of Sardinia and the *talayot* towers of Minorca (**42**), which are also fitted into the sequence. Christian concludes

> *It is unquestionable that under slight modification these towers are to be found in the islands of the Mediterranean and its shores, on the Atlantic shores of Spain, France England, Scotland, Ireland, and we are not aware that they have been found in any of the inland countries of Europe. We hope this point will attract some attention from antiquarians.* (p31)

She believed that the art of building was acquired from the Phoenicians.

The 'diffusionist' ideas of cultures spreading north-westwards from a central European homeland proposed by Gordon Childe and Christopher Hawkes have come and gone since Christian's day. Today it is generally accepted that there is such a linked distribution of 'Atlantic Round Houses' (ie brochs and duns) in the coastal areas of Scotland, Ireland, northern Spain and possibly the Mediterranean islands. Modern scholars do now see the 'stone fort' or Atlantic round house tradition as a distinctive Atlantic Iron Age culture which embraces Atlantic Scotland, Ireland, and

44 *Model of the broch of Mousa, showing imagined orthostats (Smith Art Gallery and Museum, Stirling)*

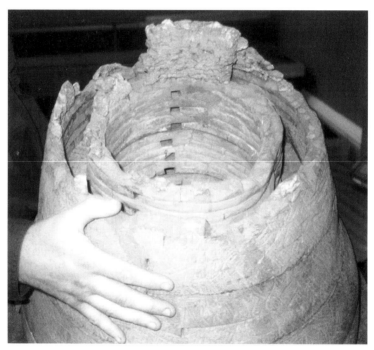

45 *Model of the broch of Mousa, showing the closing at the top (Smith Art Gallery and Museum, Stirling)*

the north-west Iberian peninsular (Harding 1990). She can be credited with being amongst the first to recognise this.

The final problem Christian considers is the roofing or top closure of brochs. Her eventual solution does not appear in print until the publication of her penultimate book in 1894, *"What Mean these Stones?"*. Here she takes for her prototypes the two brochs or duns in Glenelg, Inverness-shire (**2–3**). Her source is Gordon's *Itinerarium* of 1727. Christian relies on Gordon's assurance that, 'Living in an age of robust fighting men, all unknowing of "Macintoshes" and umbrellas, [he] at once thought the tower was for such warriors and their beds'. Christian's conclusion is that the cavity walls of the brochs definitely did close at the top and that there was possibly a corbelled roof above, which completely closed off the top of the tower. (For the reasoning behind this see cap 7). So convinced was she that the cavity walls did close at the top that she made a papier-mâché model to prove her theory (**44–5**).

So we finally come to the great Broch of Mousa (**42**), the tallest of the surviving brochs:

> In it we do not see a close of the cavity and stair; but it is generally agreed
> that it is now shorn of ten feet of its original height, and hence we can, from its
> appearance draw no conclusions.

However when Christian came to make a model of this broch (preserved at the Smith Art Gallery and Museum, Stirling), she had no doubts any more about the closure of the wall cavity. It is clearly shown, as are the nonexistent orthostats at the base of the tower. Yet her drawing (**42**), presumably done at the time of her visit, does not show the orthostats but does show a ring of stones outside which she claims no one else has noticed. But she is not the first and will not be the last to be carried away by imaginative convictions and to alter the evidence to suit her theory. The nineteenth-century German biologist Kaemerer provides a contemporary parallel: he was so convinced of the transmission of inherited characteristics that he painted spots on beetles to prove his point. Margaret Meade, whose *Coming of Age in Samoa* is now generally accepted as being factually unreliable and imaginative in parts, continued the practice more recently. There was a Belgian scientist, Professor René Blondlot, who firmly believed that N-rays, produced by looking through a prism, made previously invisible objects give out a luminescent glow in the dark (Collins 2002). However, Christian truly believed in what she said and wrote, and she was interpreting from meticulously observed facts, yet the evidence of her own drawings proves that she deceived herself in the service of her own truth.

It is fascinating how this able, highly intelligent woman who measured and recorded everything so exactly could be so disastrously wrong in some ways due to an inflexible mindset. She lacked today's chronological perspectives but she did recognise many analogies and looked beyond the narrow bounds of Scotland.

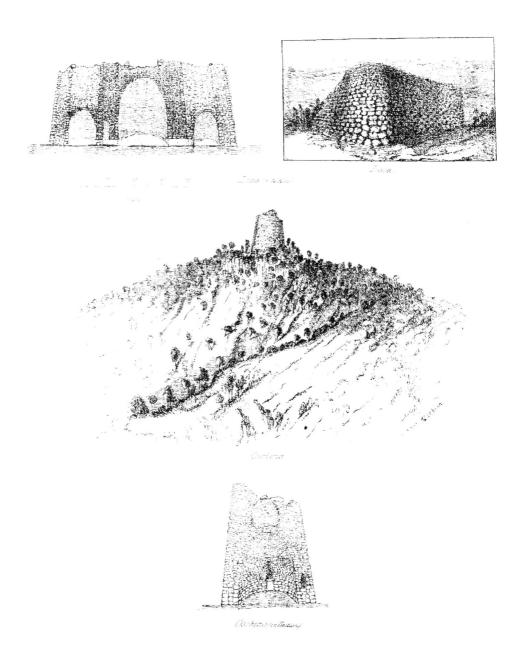

46 *Sardinian* nuraghi*: Losa (top) section and elevation; and view of Oschino with section below (1881, pl 2)*

6   Trips to Brittany, Sardinia and Rome

The two later archaeological books do show some signs of the lady's ageing, as her opinions and prejudices become more entrenched. Christian was most probably already in her sixties when she first went abroad to Brittany, Italy and Sardinia. The resulting book shows a more relaxed and self-assured personality. It contains much more anecdotal and descriptive material than her earlier work; it also reads more like a diary of enjoyable trips abroad and, as such, makes for interesting reading.

The earlier of the two was privately and, surprisingly, anonymously published in 1881, the only clue to its author being in the title, *Chips From Old Stones. By the author of "Hill forts and stone circles of ancient Scotland"*. It covers her visits to the Sardinian *nuraghi*; the dolmens, stone rows and passage graves of Brittany; Rome; Callanish stone circle on Lewis in the Outer Hebrides; Pictish houses and a return visit to Bennachie, back in northern Scotland. Her ability to travel was certainly in no way diminished in her later years, although it must have become easier with the advent of the railways.

The dedication is to the Rev Edward L Barnwell of, Melksham House, Wiltshire, who gave her the run of his library and the benefit of his own antiquarian lore. The book is rather a hotchpotch of things which she probably wished to record before her demise, as she was by then over seventy. It starts well with chapters on Sardinia and Brittany but then rather deteriorates into a series of disconnected observations intended to prove her main ideas. But there is a good chapter on Bennachie (see above, cap 4).

Sardinia

The first chapter, on the Sardinian *nuraghi*, opens in her typically aggressive manner, designed to put most folks' backs up before she even starts! These *nuraghi* are immediately claimed as prehistoric defensive towers which show a marked similarity to the Scottish brochs:

> *It must often have been remarked by those who are in the habit of reading treatises (great or small) on antiquities, that their authors, while sufficiently able to describe the objects they have seen, are, from the narrow field of their observation (it may be a parish or a county), but ill furnished with a basis on which to found rational theories, and yet that the men who are in possession of the fewest facts are those who indulge in the greatest amount of theory.* (p1)

She gets even more cantankerous in her old age; **she** knew better than other authors as her theories were based on fact and her own exact observations and measurements. What she considers the best book on the subject of *nuraghi* is by De La Marmora

(1839) but he could not even draw and had to get another to do it for him, while she herself was an artist. But De La Marmora did recognise an affinity between the *nuraghi* and Scottish towers. Strangely, however, Christian seems to have missed the most significant Italian archaeologist of the nineteenth century, Giovanni Spano, who published a major paper on Sardinian *nuraghi* in 1854 and another, very important one in 1871 – maybe she did not like Spano or approve of his views!

Thus this venerable lady arrived at Cagliari in Sardinia, and she shows very considerable descriptive ability of the town and environs when she lets herself go. Her account reads rather like a travel brochure:

> *The view from the heights of Cagliari is an exceedingly grand one. Looking out from the shade of its trees, we have the blue Mediterranean full in sight on one side; a creek stretches far inland on another; there are several little lakes on a third; and when the sun shines out in strength on all these waters, the scene is indeed one of dazzling beauty. Again, on another side is a far-reaching plain, studded with villages, gleaming and lighting up the green expanse. Beyond these stands a goodly array of mountains. ...*
>
> *As for Cagliari itself, it stands on a rock of gentle ascent from the landward side, but presenting a bold cliff towards the sea. Its streets are very steep as they climb the ascent; but they are much broader than those of most Italian cities, and , what is better still, they are much cleaner. The houses of the humbler classes are furnished in a substantial, though somewhat clumsy, style, and seemed clean and orderly. The middle and upper classes generally live in "flats" of houses, like those of Edinburgh a hundred years ago. The shops are fairly supplied with goods, and there is one excellent restaurant; but as few travellers visit this city, the hotel accommodation is wretched. (p2)*

Her interests in housing conditions and general public hygiene were not forgotten even when abroad.

The Sardinian antiquaries 'presided over by Cavaliere Gaetano Cara, who also is president of the Council of Education of Italy' allowed her the use of anything in the University museum or library, and she notes which 'home authorities would not have accorded'. The learned gentleman's son, Signor Alberto Cara, accompanied her on expeditions, and she is profuse in her appreciation of the hospitality of the Sardinian people generally. Access to many of the *nuraghi* was difficult because of the numerous *banditti* who occupied them, but this was not to deter the British lady antiquary. When trains were not available the party travelled in a waggonette on a road which was paved with water-rolled stones. The measure of jolting was something new even in her experience and the streams and waterworn stones added an additional hazard. 'Nevertheless the half-witted Neapolitan driver lashed his horses with a will, as if he were still on the Toledo.'

After a day of looking at *nuraghi* the driver was distinctly the worse for alcohol and the party wisely spent the night as guests of a wealthy villager. Next day there was a wedding *festa* and Christian remarks that in the Church 'rude and ugly were the pictures on its walls and one could not help thinking that the Virgin Mary does not see her own likenesses, and perhaps one may add, nor hear the prayers addressed to them'. Is this an example of a possible sense of humour or is it the strict Calvinist upbringing manifesting itself? One would like to believe the former. She also refers to 'the feeble sound of the Italian bagpipe' as opposed to the robust Scottish one, of course.

In further anecdotal aspects of her visit she describes how the *Guardia* (a necessary accompaniment because of danger from the *banditti*) had to help her across a wide ravine which was declared impossible to cross, in order to reach the exact spot for a drawing of a particular *nuraghe*, Oschino (**46**). This minor difficulty did not however deter her. But

> *the glare was distressing to the sketcher. "Guardia" had under his charge the crimson umbrella of the good Sindico* [her host], *and he was requested to put it up, to shade the artist. He made the attempt again and again, but failed. Forthwith sprung up from beneath a bush a small urchin, whose presence had hitherto been unobserved, and, being an instructed youth, he saw into the mystery of rearing the umbrella. The spreading shade was thus obtained, and the pencil did its work. The shade was no longer needed, and the umbrella was ordered to be put down; but this requirement was again beyond the skill of "Guardia," and the more learned youngster had to show the way.* (p9)

This is surely, despite the differences of usage, an example of the fact that Christian possessed a truly ironic and sensitive sense of humour.

There were trains available, but Christian opined that they were run for punctuality and not for the whims of the passengers. So one journey back from Paulo Latini to Orestia had to be by a 'diligence' and the party had to wait several days before there was space for at least some of them. But a few hours after they finally departed,

> *there came to the door of the Sindico a peasant, who had walked from a distant part of the country, his sole and earnest desire a being to see the lady who had been seen wandering among the Nuraghi, as he believed she had wonderful powers, and would be able to cure him of epilepsy, with which he was sorely afflicted.*

Christian's reaction is not altogether sympathetic,

> *Sorcery is in these parts more believed in than antiquarianism.* (p11)

Christian's reception on her final return to Cagliari was in the form of an invitation to join the local antiquaries in an imminent expedition. Sadly, however, she had to decline because she had run out of funds, and storms on the Mediterranean were

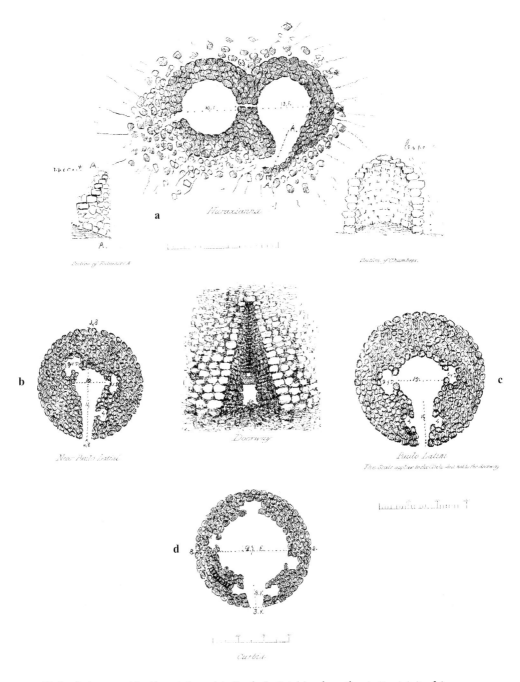

47 *Sardinian* nuraghi*: Nuraxi Anna (***a***); Paulo Latini (***c***)and another in its vicinity (***b***); Carbia (***d***) (1881, pl 1)*

foretold. But she contrasted 'the politeness of the Sardinian Antiquarian Society in striking contrast to our doings in Scotland'.

Dealing with the archaeology, Christian noted that the *nuraghi* had two or more storeys with just one high window, as in her interpretation of Maeshowe (see cap 5, p63f). Also the doors were shut from the inside and not from the outside. In these respects they clearly resembled Scottish brochs in her opinion.

She travelled a considerable distance, 100 miles, northwards to Oristano where the railway terminated, 'and posted to the land of the nuraghi, Paulo Latini. In the distant view nuraghi were here and there visible – lone, desolate towers scattered over a waste wilderness unapproachable by anyone'. But, at last, one, Carbia, was seen by the roadside. It was in a morass with a stream wandering through it 'but difficulties of hill and bog must be faced, for this was evidently a good specimen'. A plan of this particular *nuraghe* is illustrated (**47d**), and Christian notes that it was similar to the Oschino one. The ground plan she thought strongly resembled the Broch at Coldoch in Perthshire (see cap 4, p34).

The visit to Oschino was again led by a local *Guardia*.

> *Rough and thorny was the way. Every step was from one rude stone to another, the country being a wide-spread table-land which is thickly strewn with boulders of all sorts and sizes, and also covered with the most impenetrable jungle, in the midst of which the Nuraghi stand.* (p8)

The ruinous Oschino *nuraghe* (**46**), she reckoned, could have stood 37 feet or more. As the lower chamber was about 27 feet in height there must have been a substantial chamber above it. This is the evidence on which she bases her views that Maeshowe and other 'brochs' originally had two chambers, one on top of the other. When she tried to ascend the stairs in the ruins to get exact measurements the *Guardia* pulled her back just as the coachman had done at Dun Carloway on Lewis (see cap 7). The weakness of men! At another *nuraghe*, Losa (**46**), where the stairway remained for 35 feet, she had better luck. 'It is a very difficult thing to climb, but I did it', she says with pride.

Like the brochs, the *nuraghi* had either no windows or only very small ones high up. The doorposts were similar in both types of monument and the doors were designed to be closed from within. And what need was there for windows in a society which did not need light as we do and to whom defence and safety were the primary considerations? After all, windows only let in the cold and had to be boarded up against it. Thus the *nuraghi* were definitely intended to be lived in as the Sardinians naturally concluded.

> *Yet, strange to say, our Scottish antiquaries can look at the numerous buildings of their own land, whose doors are* exactly similar, *and yet they do not recognise the force of this argument, but continue to characterise every dark chamber as*

a tomb. ... It almost amounts to a rule, that the more ancient the human dwelling is the fewer windows will be found in its walls. (pp8–9)

Christian noted that groups of *nuraghi* were gathered together on flat platforms which had previously been considered to be solid bedrock. However, with her aptitude for appreciation of minute detail, she claimed to have discovered that while the individual dwellings were indeed founded on bedrock the spaces between them had been filled in with small stones to give the appearance of a level platform.

Following the premise that the fewer the windows the greater the antiquity of the dwelling, Christian concludes that the dolmens of Brittany and Scotland are the oldest type of dwellings (see next section). Next come the *nuraghi* of Sardinia, the *talayote* of the Balearic Islands and then the brochs of Scotland, and the latest are the earliest baronial towers such as Old Wick Castle in Caithness.

The *nuraghi* she visited were: Nuraxi Anna, Nuraghe Ortu and a 'grotto' nearby, *nuraghi* near Paolo Latini (Oschino, Arbiddera, Carbia, Silonus, Losa, Cuada and others); quite an achievement, but accomplished with the kind assistance of local antiquaries. She produced plans and artistic drawings; but her observations did not add a great deal to the knowledge current at that time. However, she clearly enjoyed herself and the challenge of the *banditti* and revelled in the appreciation of Sardinian colleagues, which was not accorded to her at home; presumably because at home they knew her better!

Brittany

The second chapter of *Chips* is on Brittany, where Christian went to see for herself the dolmens and stone avenues. She had done her reading of La Lomand (1853), Lukis (nd), and J Mahé (1825), and she had discussed the sites with the Rev Barnwell, but it seems as though she went with her mind already made up and then looked for the evidence to confirm her ideas.

She starts well enough with a general topographic survey. In this she notes that the granite plateau on which the monuments stand is only covered with a thin layer of soil, and points out that the monuments are constructed from the granite which weathers naturally into the huge monoliths. Those who think of the dolmens as stone tables (*daul-table* and *mein-stone*) are soundly berated because these huge stones could never have been supported except by a surrounding mound. So far so good! But then her theories and imagination come into play; yet there is a consistent mad logic in her thinking.

She entertained the firm belief that the uprights of the dolmens could not be deeply buried because of the thin soil covering above the hard granite. She thought they stood 'as nine-pins on a board'. So the method of construction she suggests for these structures was as follows: the mounds were built first, with a hole left open in the

Loc Mariaker

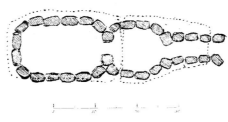

Table aux Marchands

Kercado Interior

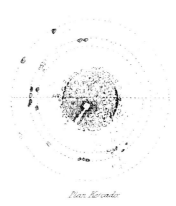

Plan Kercado

48 *Brittany: Table des Marchands, Locmariaquer; Kercado dolmen, Carnac (1881, pl 3)*

centre; the pillars or uprights were then lowered in and the large capstones subsequently placed on top before the mound was finally covered over. The mounds were gradually denuded by the ubiquitous farmers who needed good topsoil for their poor granitic fields. She is at least monotonously consistent in that it is the farmers who are to answer for the present state of prehistoric monuments by their continual removal of stones and topsoil. But if it is indeed the case that the uprights were not buried deeply in the soil, she fails to answer adequately the question why more of them have not fallen down.

Christian's theory is that dolmens were built to resemble caves and they are therefore 'artificial caves'. She quotes examples on Boreray, a small island in the

St Kilda group, where people lived in caves within living memory and some 'croups' or beds were still visible in them in 1862. Most probably, therefore, the dolmens were houses for the living and not for the dead at all, and on the authority of Lukis she cites examples of domestic debris found in them such as flints, gold bands, spindle whorls and necklaces. Some houses in Shetland in her day still had no windows and the Picts, she believed, had lived in souterrains or earth houses. After all, a relative of hers (? her brother) living in Bengal, built houses with windows for his workers but they still preferred to live in caves! If dolmens were indeed tombs, she asks, what had happened to the houses for the living? It was inconceivable to her that the houses for the living should not have survived when those for the dead still stood. She then cites the Bible where there is ample evidence that ancient peoples built towers, cities, palaces and temples all of which were more important than their tombs. The passage graves so closely resembled the Scottish souterrains that they also were clearly dwellings rather than tombs.

The dolmen at Kercado had most of its massive stones still in place and it was surrounded by a well-built circular mass or tower of stone 60 feet in diameter and about 12 feet in height (**48**). Close by was a handsome château surrounded by tall garden walls and the owner admitted that many of the stones for this wall had come from the dolmen mound. 'Would there be no chambers in that upper portion of the building which has been removed?', she asks, just like the *nuraghi* and the brochs. She is certainly not averse to adapting facts to suit theories, the vice she so soundly berates in others. In other words these structures (passage graves in modern parlance), are really the remains of defended dwellings, probably with an upper chamber. There is a ground plan of this dolmen, clearly drawn with a compass (cf **7**).

So-called sculpturings
In the interior of the dolmens she found very feeble scratchings as compared with the bold Scottish ones. This seems strange to us as she did visit the Table des Marchands and probably Gavrinis, both of which have splendid, deeply pecked, scroll and circle patterns. She would, of course, not have had the advantage of a powerful modern torch, but this seems another example of basing some at least of her conclusions upon preconceived ideas and prejudices.

The theories get even more outrageous, if possible, when she comes to discuss the famous Carnac alignments. These stone avenues she saw as possible remains of villages, following her obsession that all prehistoric structures were originally dwellings for the living. Thus it followed that stone rows could be the remains of dolmens (ie dwellings) which were once covered by mounds. She cites the observation of Mahé that the stones in these rows were originally contiguous: '*Elles se touchent commes des soldats dont on fait le revue*' (J Mahé *Antiquites de Morbihan,* 1825). But the local farmers, again, had removed the smaller intervening stones as they had likewise removed the soil covering the mounds. The numerous large stones lying around were, most probably, the remains of the roofs of these dolmens or rather dwellings. She noted that the soil was very thin (only a foot deep at the post office court) but everywhere there were mounds of seaweed to make new soil. If the soil was so precious that farmers had to resort to making it artificially, then clearly ancient people would have taken advantage of the mounds of earth covering the dolmens for use on their fields, just as they had taken the stone for their houses. She says that Caesar, a meticulous observer, makes no mention in his account of his campaigns in Brittany, of the long rows of standing stones which to her is evidence that they must still have been covered by mounds of earth in his day.

At Carnac, Menec and other stone avenues she visited, Christian noticed, as had others before her, that the alignments had stone circles attached, or rather squares with rounded corners, which were perhaps originally fortified strongholds (**49**). And the alignments draw closer together as they near these circles and the ends furthest away from them were spread out fanwise. 'Well, if one were to suppose those circles to be the remains of forts, and the stone lines to be those of towns or villages, the gathering around a place of defence would be natural enough' (p22). This is a logical conclusion given her premises and perhaps no odder than that the avenues were erected by prehistoric megalomaniac dictators, as someone else has suggested!

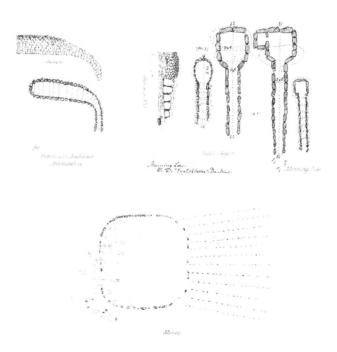

49 *Brittany: Roche Guyon passage grave compared with one at Mininglow, Derbyshire, and with an Aberdeenshire souterrain; below Menec alignments (1881, pl 4)*

50 *Callanish, Lewis: plan of standing stones and plan of central chamber compared with Camster Cairns, Caithness and Kercado, Brittany (1881, pl 5)*

Callernish (Callanish)

Back in Scotland she visited, in 1876, the great stone circle of Callanish with its associated avenues on the Isle of Lewis in the Outer Hebrides (**50**). Here she notes that MacCulloch, who visited in 1819, says that a local told him that the lines of stones were once continuous walls. These 'walls', she notes, are connected with circles as she had observed in Brittany. So were the circles originally defensive structures she asks? The circle stands on a ridge with military capabilities and is surrounded with precipices and sea lochs. Inside the great circle were the remains of two dolmens or ancient dwellings and these she compares with the Kercado dolmen.

She confuses souterrains with passage graves and chambered tombs; but she had at least thought. Incidentally she had clearly not visited Mininglow in Derbyshire as her drawing is quite inaccurate (**49**). She ends, characteristically: '*Nota bene.—The distance between stone and stone of the Callernish group was measured by me.*' (p25) So who could argue with that? The rest of this book mentions rings of stones in Aberdeenshire which, to her, are of course the bases of brochs, and she mentions that she had even heard of some comparable rings in Iceland although she never actually went there.

It does appear that her theories became even more deeply entrenched as she approached old age, which is sad because so few antiquarians of the period seem to have actually visited and measured as many sites as she did.

This section of *Chips* concludes with two quite unrelated items. Was Christian including these thoughts simply to make sure they got into print before her demise?

Of cairns in Caithness.

The horned cairns of Ormigail (Ulbster) and Camster, Caithness, she again regards as ancient dwellings, of course (see Feachem 1977, 44). The whole group, which is situated on an eminence, she sees as the remains of a hamlet 'the rude homes of our rude forefathers'. The sepulchral interpretation, as proposed by Mr Anderson, she rejects. It could have no application, as the dead need no wall or moat 'which apparently surrounds this site', and which moat she had observed. The views of Shearer entirely concur with her own as he believed that these cairns had been human habitations. Indeed a local told her that one line of stones was put up quite recently to dry clothes. This seems a very arduous way of doing things!

Foro Romano

In her later years Christian did visit Rome. In the Forum she set to work to draw some 'cup' marks on the steps of the Senate building, taking no notice of two policemen who asked her to desist. Eventually she learns from a 'captain of police' that she needs 'the sanction of a certain official (whose designation I forget). Rome is not yet very free, when an artist cannot do a drawing of her stones without leave!' (p38)

She compared the marks to Scottish cup-marks, demonstrating a trace of the Celt in Rome. But her drawing (**51**), of course, clearly demonstrates that the pattern of depressions served what is now well known for an ancient board game. She either did not register, or chose to ignore the phallic symbol, accurately drawn but not commented upon.

In the middle of all these odds and ends there is an excellent short chapter on the Mither Tap of Bennachie (see above, cap 4). It is very well observed and rational in its conclusions.

Altogether, *Chips* is a mixture of observation, facts and mere notes randomly gathered at the end to perpetuate her thoughts. She was seventy-one after all when the book was published, and cannot have foreseen many productive years yet to come, and may have been anxious to leave nothing unrecorded.

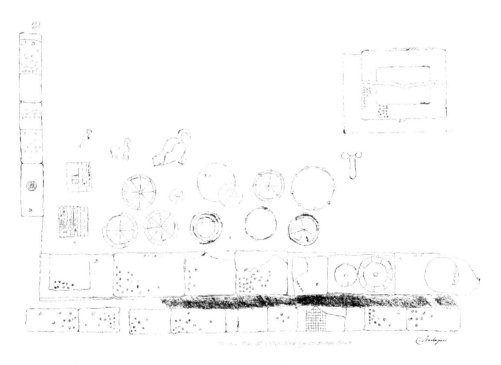

51 *Rome: plan of cup-markings on the Forum (1881, pl 8)*

7 *"What Mean These Stones?"*, 1894.

This was Christian's penultimate book, published when she was 83 and dedicated to her cousin Hugh Kerr Colville, Esq, Bellaport, Shropshire, who was to be the chief mourner at her funeral. It is not surprising that she has little new to say in this volume except to reiterate her firmly held views. However she does append one significant new theory; namely that the hollow walls of the brochs were closed at the top.

She starts with a quotation from the Bible, in whose literal truth she believed. She takes her title from Joshua 4.7:

> *"What mean these twelve stones?" and the divine answer to the question is "Then ye shall answer them that the waters of Jordan were cut off before the Ark of the Covenant of the Lord; when it passed over Jordan the waters of Jordan were cut off: and these stones shall be for a memorial unto the Children of Israel for ever."*

This particular quotation is used to demonstrate that stones have been set up from time immemorial and no one really knows why. One suggestion, made by an English antiquary years ago, was that Stonehenge had been 'spewed up from the earth; but he does not mention at what date this sore fit of our mother earth's sickness had occurred, so we have only his word for it' (p11). This she curtly dismisses as on a par with all the various druidical theories started off by John Aubrey. She reiterates her theory that the recumbent stones were not altars but lintels of stone brochs. She is equally scornful of the theory that stone circles were sepulchral monuments just because bones were found in them; after all the plentiful stones of the decayed brochs would have been suitable burial sites to protect the dead from beasts of prey. Again a Bible quotation comes to her aid, Samuel 25.1, which shows that it was customary to bury the dead in their own houses.

A fellow antiquary, the Rev J C Michie, is quoted at length as he agrees with her that individual standing stones did not have their bases deeply embedded in the soil. She was of the opinion that the cap or roofing stones of the dolmens of Brittany were sometimes re-erected as standing stones; current thought suggests the contrary to have been the case, namely that the standing stones were sometimes reused as cap stones for dolmens.

The only new idea put forward in this penultimate book is based on observations made by herself and the Rev Macrae at the Broch of Carloway on the Isle of Lewis. As a result she is convinced that the double-skinned and therefore hollow walls of brochs joined up at the top and were thus closed there. Her sketch of the Dun Telve tower at Glenelg illustrates this (**52**). There are several towers or brochs in Glenelg of which two, Dun Telve and Dun Troddan (Feachem 1977, 163–4; Ritchie & Ritchie,

154–5) still stand to a height which is second only to the great broch of Mousa. There are two unpublished drawings by Christian of Dun Telve and Dun Troddan, one annotated in her own hand 'copy from Gordon's Iter' (**2–3**). In the one of Dun Telve the gap between the walls narrows dramatically but does not quite close. Gordon's *Itinerarium* was published in 1726, so the drawings, which Christian copied from him, must have been made some time earlier when he visited several towers in Glenelg, 'and he had actually seen them', unlike some others as Christian is careful to stress. It is possible that she had not actually seen them, but took her evidence from Gordon. There is a careful drawing by Henry Dryden, dated 1866, which shows Dun Telve with walls merging at the top. Much later photographs taken by Euan Mackie and Dennis Harding show that the walls certainly 'merge' at the top but now they are partially collapsed. All this material is preserved at the NMRS in Edinburgh, and on this evidence it does seem that Christian may have had a valid point, to the extent that the walls of some brochs may have originally joined at the top as she shows in her sketch of Dun Carloway and in her model of the Broch of Mousa (**45**).

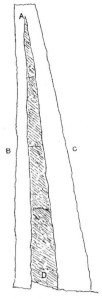

A Closing in of cavity
B Inner wall
C Outer wall
D Cavity in wall

52 *Dun Troddan, Inver-ness-shire: section of wall showing cavity*

Describing Castle Troddan, Gordon states that

> *the perpendicular height is 33ft and the thickness of both walls (including the cavity) no more than 12ft, and the cavity itself hardly wide enough for two men to walk abreast. The whole height of the fabric is divided into four parts or storeys, separated from each other by thin floorings of flat stones, which knit the two walls together, and run quite round the building. And there have even been winding stairs of the same flat stones betwixt wall and wall up to the top. The walls grow narrower by degrees until they **close at the top**.* (p39)

A rough drawing by Christian illustrates the top closure which would have provided dry sleeping places in the galleries for the fighting men with no waterproof clothing (**52**). Now if Gordon is indeed describing Dun Troddan then he **may have seen the stones** which closed the top before they were removed. Visiting in 1722 Thomas Pennant noted that 'some Goth purloined the top seven and a half feet under the pretence of applying the material to certain public buildings'. Dun Troddan today stands only 25 feet high.

Christian enlarges on this theory of the top closure of the broch walls, developed and reinforced by several visits to Dun Carloway on the Isle of Lewis. She explains how the inside wall of the structure was used for support and the outer one gradually sloped inwards. Thus dry sleeping quarters were provided for the stout defenders and explains why there are no windows in the towers; after all why have them if they did not need to see out? These towers were provided for defence and not offence. Other sleeping quarters were provided on the ground floor which could be adequately roofed from internal ledges. In fact here she was observing what we now call a wheelhouse structure built within the brochs, some of which may have been contemporary with the original structure and some later. She thought that the towers were not entirely roofed over to allow for the escape of smoke.

The supposed precedent of closure at the top of the walls at Dun Troddan was now applied to Dun Carloway on Lewis. Christian's views were strongly endorsed by the resident minister, the Reverend Macrae. He wrote in a letter to her that he thought the inside wall was as much for supporting the structure as for anything else and that the tower was built in a conical form meeting at the top, which would strengthen the inside wall considerably. He assured her that she could '**rest satisfied that the cavity walls did meet some distance below the summit of the tower**'. Many others who had actually **seen** the structure agreed with him, including the Rev Dr Maclaughlin. What higher authorities could one hope for than the testimony of two Reverend gentlemen?

After quoting the Rev Macrae at great length, Christian concludes that there could be no doubt about the closure of these cavity walls at the top. Of this fact she felt quite sure 'although a mere woman and unworthy of being a member of any antiquarian society'. The fact that she had to be content with being a 'mere' Lady Associate was perpetually festering.

We may leave her at this point on a personal visit to the Carloway Broch. When the artist (herself) had finished her drawings, she and the coachman began to mount the stair in the wall. After climbing for some time the cavity became painfully narrow and the walls thinner so that the blue sky could be seen. At this point the cabman refused to go any further but Christian had satisfied herself about the closure of the walls. Now that the evidence has disappeared, who can say categorically that she was not right?

"What Mean these Stones?" concludes on the very positive note that, of course, not a single idol was found in any of these brochs.

> *May we not then, indulge in the hope that they [our forefathers], still in simple form, were following the worship of the God of Abraham, who was not suffered to build an altar to the Most high, and knew no temple save the blue heavens? That they were men of courage, determined to hold and keep their own, these buildings and weapons found among them sufficiently attest; and that they were no predatory folk, but a home-abiding generation.*

A CATALOGUE RAISONNÉ OF THE

BRITISH MUSEUM COLLECTION

of Rubbings from Ancient Sculptured Stones

A CHAPTER OF SCOTLAND'S HISTORY

AS IT IS WRITTEN ON ITS ROCKS AND STONES AS
'WITH A PEN OF IRON ON THE ROCK FOR EVER,' ALSO
OF WHO IT WAS THAT DID THIS WRITING, AND
OF WHO IT WAS THAT UNDID IT

BY

CHRISTIAN MACLAGAN

AUTHOR OF 'HILL FORTS AND STONE CIRCLES'
'CHIPS FROM OLD STONES,' ETC.

EDINBURGH: DAVID DOUGLAS

CASTLE STREET

1898

53 *Title page of Christian's catalogue of rubbings*

8   The 'rubbings'

In this chapter we now get to grips with another of Christian's major preoccupations: her 'rubbings' of Pictish symbol stones, Christian crosses, gravestones and medieval tombstones. She made these from at least the 1870s, and possibly from an earlier date, in parallel with her study of other antiquities. Her 'rubbings' of the surface features of the stones were done using an undisclosed technique which she herself had developed after failing to succeed with other recommended methods.

Others had drawn artistic and later increasingly accurate representations of the stones which were then reproduced by engraving or lithography. Photography had been experimented with, and sometimes excellent prints were obtained, but reproducing these images on the page was problematic as photolithography, then at an early stage of its development, was not yet capable of giving wholly satisfactory results. Rubbing was regarded by some as the most accurate method of representing the sculpture, and therefore superior to drawing, a contention which led to much lively debate amongst Scots antiquaries about the respective merits of drawing and rubbing.

Christian's first published paper on the subject of carved stone was on the Pictish and early Christian 'sculpturings' on the walls of the Wemyss Caves, Fife (1874; Ritchie & Ritchie, 107–9). She characteristically appreciates the setting too:

> We visited this cave at noontide of a day, hot with midsummer's sunshine. Under the cool shade of the cave the cows of two neighbouring villages assembled; by and by the village maidens also came to milk them. Here and there long lines of sunbeams, bursting into the gloom through the lofty archways, lighted up a singular scene of pastoral beauty.[7]

This article was followed by another, 'Sculptured stones with symbols at Rhynie' (1879) (**54**). Others followed (1882/83/86) and in 1890 she was confident enough to publish a paper in which she attempted to set out stylistic differences between the sculptures of the early western Christian church (Iona-based) and the eastern, or more strongly Pictish east. From 1883 to 1901, the year of her death, she exhibited her 'rubbings' on at least four occasions in Glasgow and Stirling, which received some acclaim. After a lecture given to the Stirling Antiquarian Society in 1895 on the subject of sculptured stones at St Andrews, Mr George Lawson said in appreciation

> After what has been said, it will not be necessary to insist on the inestimable value of these monuments to us as a nation. We have awakened, thanks to the teaching of many cultured men and women, to an appreciation of art and archaeology. But this, as yet, applies chiefly to the art of lands save our own and we leave those indigenous monuments of which I have spoken to the mercies of the weather and wayfarer. May I urge anew that in their ornamentation we

54 *Wood engravings of Christian's drawings of two Pictish symbol stones at Rhynie, Aberdeenshire: Rhynie 6 (left) and Rhynie 5 (1881a, p12, figs 1 & 2)*

> *have the teaching material for a school of national design. The preservation of which I have spoken would be largely brought about by the multiplication of copies of the representations. (Trans Stirling 17)*

He went on to compliment Miss Maclagan on bringing the art of rubbings to perfection and on the completion of her work. He was sure that she agreed with him that it was regrettable that her collection was in London rather than Edinburgh. The sad reality is that to this day these not inconsiderable images still languish in the British Library practically unknown.

Romilly Allen and Joseph Anderson, the generally acknowledged authorities on early medieval carved stones in Scotland, in their impressive corpus of 1903, *The Early Christian Monuments of Scotland* (*ECMS*), mention (ii, p184) Christian's description and illustration of the two Rhynie stones, nos 5 and 6 (1881a) (**54**), but of her 'rubbings', there is no reference whatsoever. She herself expresses bitterness in her books that the Society of Antiquaries of Scotland did not appreciate or even acknowledge her work.

Amongst the early illustrators, Gordon sketched the monuments himself on site and these drawings were then transcribed by the engraver on to copper plates (1726). Pennant took an artist with him on his later journeys (1772). Cordiner, a trained artist, drew the stones but his illustrations are idiosyncratic and imaginative (1788–95). Chalmers also employed an artist and he was the first in the field to appreciate the possibilities of the now popular medium of lithography (1848). The Spalding Club also employed lithographic artists to illustrate their two-volume corpus edited by John Stuart (1856–67).

ECMS is a truly masterly compendium of early medieval carved stones both in Scotland and beyond. All the various motifs are considered, classified and illustrated by clear drawings. The stones themselves are illustrated by photographs or by drawings done in a clear diagrammatic style. At this time photography began to be more widely available, and was the recommended recording medium. Where possible, it was used in *ECMS*, even for the drawings, which were made from photographically reduced rubbings. Allen and Anderson's work is an excellent, meticulously organised source-book. In contrast, Christian Maclagan's catalogue is rambling, episodic and punctuated by her own personal prejudices, including a long section on the dissolution of the monasteries in relation to the fate of many of the stones she recorded. But the 'rubbing' technique involved a unique immediacy of reproduction, and she did make all of the 'rubbings' herself. She herself was the 'artist' as she constantly asserts, and she naturally visited all the monuments personally.

Spanning a period from the Bronze Age to the sixteenth century, the scope of her 'rubbings' is very wide, covering mainly Pictish and early Christian sculpture and medieval graveslabs, but also cup-and-ring-marked stones, ogham inscriptions and runes for good measure. In other words, the *Catalogue Raisonné* (*CR*) published in 1898 in her 89th year, was an effort to record, describe and systematise her work on sculptured stones over possibly almost half a century, and, together with the exhibitions, is a last effort to record and organize her work before her final demise. How great the task she undertook emerges both from the *Catalogue* and from the *Stirling Observer's* obituary:

> *The rubbings were done in the most adverse conditions after incredible difficulties in reaching the spots. Yet these difficulties she never mentioned except to laugh and only from her devoted friend, the late Miss Colvin, who accompanied her on many expeditions, could any adequate idea of them be gathered.*

The book is a human document, full of humour, anecdote and historical snippets, very much in the style of the Arthur Mee county guides which can still be used as a less thorough but more enjoyable accompaniment to Pevsner guides. The full title of the book is:

> *A Catalogue Raisonné of the British Museum Collection of Rubbings from Ancient sculptured Stones, A Chapter of Scotland's History as it is written on its rocks and Stones as 'with a pen of iron on the rock forever,' also of who it was that did this writing, and of who it was that undid it.*[8]

It describes the nature of the stones she has recorded, their geographical location and her difficulties in recording them. She then continues with a lengthy discussion of the final fate of the monasteries and churches where many of these stones are located, but this is basically a diverting accompaniment to the detailed catalogue of her 'rubbings', none of which are reproduced in the volume in any form (or indeed in any other publication). However the book is far more than just a catalogue as it records her problems in uncovering some of the stones, her adventures along the way, the romantic settings of many of the churchyards and monasteries, snippets of Scottish history, a recognition of different styles of art and her views on the general disrespect accorded to medieval women.

In the Preface, Christian acknowledges the particular help of two valued friends, Miss Pope and Dr Nicoll, RN (both of whom were remembered in her will), but she stresses that the 'rubbings' are all her own unassisted work and are taken by a method which she herself invented. Initially she sought 'some instruction in the art of taking impressions of stone on paper' from the official at the Edinburgh Antiquarian Museum who was 'in charge of the few sculptured stones' –

> *His reply was, "Just spread your paper over the stones and rub it with grass or docken leaves." I was a mere novice, and he an LL.D., and it was natural to give his advice a trial. This was done in the ancient churchyard of Kildalton. But it was in another way and on another day that the rubbings were done from the stones of this place that are now in the British Museum. I mention the above chiefly for the purpose of distinctly affirming that* my *way of doing rubbings is simply my own invention.* (CR, Preface [iii])

She was so proud of her method that she resolutely refused to divulge it to anyone. Christian hoped that the beauty and power of many of the designs 'might give a lesson to our modern art-workers in stone, wood, silver, and gold, and tend to restore a better style of workmanship and a purer taste in art conceptions'. In other words back to our pure and noble ancestors.

The present author was able to examine about a dozen of the original rubbings, the total collection of which is now in the care of the British Library, except for a few in Edinburgh (NMRS). These are taken on fairly substantial paper. For the cross-slab, Fowlis Wester 1, which is just over three metres high, she used only two pieces of paper for the main face, which suggests that she must have had rolls of about two metres in length. The rubbings seem to have been made with a mixture of brown cobbler's wax and graphite and the outlines of the figures and decoration were pencilled in, probably on the spot. Later, at home in comfort, these were touched-up and a brown or grey wash added to indicate the colour of the stone. On the Fowlis Wester rubbing one black hair still adheres to the wash. The individual sheets of paper are stuck together with the edges of the stones being painted on afterwards. The whole rubbing is backed with a stiff linen material which has been machine-stitched. The paper itself is strangely always unevenly cut.

There is a sureness of touch in the portrayal of the interlace patterns; yet oddly, these and all other figures, are highlighted and shaded as if lit from the top right instead of the usually accepted convention of top left. This may indicate the use of her left hand due to her disability. The figures are usually less satisfactorily portrayed than the interlace patterns, especially apparent in the raised medieval tomb figures which are very stiff. When she comes to the figures and symbols on the Pictish stones these are often quite crude in comparison with the figures from Iona and the west (possibly reflecting her bias towards a purer form of Christianity). Her method of showing the patterns on the sides of the flat graveslabs is ingenious, being depicted in the manner of an opened out envelope (**55**).

At this point it seems reasonable to consider what exactly Christian was aiming to produce with her 'rubbings'; were they intended as faithful representations, or as something which could be worked up with the potential of becoming works of art in their own right? I suspect that the 'rubbings' combined both aims. Stuart's 'faithful' representations, after all, had been published in 1856 (vol 1) and 1867 (vol 2), and Christian cannot have failed to know of Romilly Allen's detailed and accurate work being undertaken in the last two decades of the nineteenth century. It seems highly probable that Christian's main aim was to produce works of art. She continually refers to herself as an artist. Above all, she says that she hopes her work, in bringing to public attention the beauties of this ancient art, will be an inspiration to future generations. It does seem, consequently, that precise accuracy was not her main aim and those who dismiss her work should bear this in mind and consider the quality of the

55 *Iona, Argyll: 'rubbing' of grave-slab (96) (Stirling Libraries)*

'rubbings' on their own merits. The one of the Aberlemno churchyard stone (Aberlemno 2) is a good example of her work and a photograph is included for comparison (**56**). In her description of the stone she mistakenly identifies 'Two grinning monks meeting' at the apex of the stone, yet this feature, which in fact comprises two confronting beasts' heads, does not appear in her rubbing. Below that are two horsemen 'one of whom appears to be casting an arrow at the moon', but who is in fact wielding a sword and the object purporting to represent the moon is a discarded shield. Of the three figures on the left of the central row she says one has a long spear and 'has a hat on his head something like a Quaker's'. There is no evidence for this on the stone, whose surface is damaged at this point, and it seems likely that she got the idea from studying either or both of P A Jastrzebski's published illustrations (Chalmers 1848, pl 5; Stuart 1856, pl 71). Comparing her 'rubbing' to a photograph of the stone and to the latter, poorly-observed, illustration, shows all too clearly that the 'rubbing' owes more to the lithographed plate than to the stone itself. This is clear evidence that not only was she using the plates in publications such as *Sculptured Stones of Scotland* as an aide-memoire to writing the catalogue, but she had also previously cribbed from them when finishing off her 'rubbings'. Memory and imagination, rather than observation and considered interpretation, seem to have played a large part in creating her 'rubbings', and, coupled with her reliance on other people's often extremely inaccurate work, it is hardly surprising that her efforts are of little value to today's scholars.

56 *Aberlemno, Angus:* **a** *Christian's 'rubbing' of the reverse of Aberlemno 2 compared with* **b** *a photograph of the stone and* **c** *PA Jastrzebski's lithograph (Stuart 1856, pl 79)*

Christian's approach to cataloguing, as set out in the *Catalogue Raisonné,* was, by her standards, reasonably systematic. She divides her heterogeneous collection of material into 'Classes' thus: First Class – Cup Markings; Second Class – Symbols or Hieroglyphics [Pictish symbol stones]; Third Class – Oghams; Fourth Class – Runes; Fifth Class – Christian Art [which covers material at least up to the sixteenth century].

The 'cup markings' she thought would have originally adorned the interiors of the homes of our ancestors, that is to say stone circles and megalithic tombs in modern parlance. This adds strength to her theory that our ancestors were not nomadic and as a result preferred permanent adornments in their homes. In this section she displays her penchant for comparative approaches, by comparing her native markings, however misguidedly, to similar patterns in Seville and Rome (**51**) (see *Chips* p32). Her friend Dr Hutchinson reported that he had seen them also in India, in the Himalayas and the Deccan, and she had read of them on Easter Island in the Pacific. She cannot resist mentioning the cup-markings at Black (*sic*) Caterthun and that she was the first to notice them. This is not an example of a record of something which is now lost, as she is really referring to the stone on the White Caterthun (**57**).[9] Also she recorded cup-markings at Cairnbaan in the valley of the Crinan canal (**21**). Antiquaries had observed but a small part of this group carved on bedrock, but she peeled off a carpet-like layer of turf exposing a continuous sheet of carvings covering 48 by 12 feet. She drew 'a careful and coloured map of this find, and gave it to the Antiquarian Society of Edinburgh. But it is nowhere recorded in the Transactions of that body, to my great regret.[10] This is only one of three similar incidents.' (*CR*, 4)

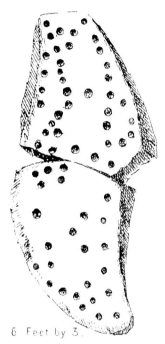

57 *White Caterthun, Angus: cup-and-ring-marked stone (1875, pl 11, detail)*

The 'hieroglyphs' or Pictish symbols, Christian concluded, had been carved with metal tools as opposed to the stone tools of the cup-mark carvings, and must therefore be later. But she does not have a great deal to say about them except that they appeared to be monumental, that they are confined to the eastern counties and that later the symbols are combined with Christian crosses. The brevity of this section confirms the theory that she was not so interested in these carvings, possibly as they could be pagan, which does not match the ideal of our noble and godly ancestors.

Ogham inscriptions receive only a brief mention (*CR*, 6) although she had studied the work of the Earl of Southesk, her scant treatment of the subject suggests that her study of the work of the noble earl cannot have been too thorough!

Runes she assigns to the seventh century and quotes in full the 'Dream of the Rood' from the Ruthwell Cross. This early Anglo-Saxon poem, attributed to Caedmon, tells the story of the Crucifixion as if the cross itself were speaking. A translated version of the poem 'as found in the library of an Austrian convent' and 'attributed to Cynewulf' is quoted in full in an appendix (*CR*, app 6, 83–5).

It is the Christian art which receives full and lengthy treatment in her book. She has, on the whole, no time for monasteries because they are nowhere sanctioned in the Bible; on the contrary

> the great Head of the Church in the Book of Books (the only true Church directory) gives no sanction for any such method of Christian life, and it had not a share in the prayer of Him who said, "I pray not that Thou shouldest take them out of the world, but that Thou shouldest keep them from the evil." (*CR*, 7)

Fortunately

> the Reformation came, and by the growing light of Holy Scripture spread by the Reformers over our country, the laity, comparing the monasteries with its sacred texts, revolted against them with deep abhorrence, and drove their inhabitants from their polluted homes (*CR*, 8);

one can almost hear John Knox here whom she greatly admired.

In her 'Fifth Class', Christian art, she identified five schools. The earliest was that found at Whithorn, the foundation of St Ninian, who started his mission in the Solway Firth area in AD397 and founded a monastery there. This she called 'St Ninian's School' (**58**).

Next in chronological order, and pre-eminent in Christian's eyes, was the 'Iona School' of which she made more than 50 rubbings in all. She starts this section with a history of St Columba. The chroniclers told that he found the Island heathen but, apparently,

> Columba never preached against idol-worship simply because ... he found no existence of it in Scotland'. No 'antiquarian searchers' in this country had found 'one heathen idol, or even any figure of one, graven on its many rocks'; indeed it was not until the 'early chroniclers ... had fallen under the teaching of Rome that they had learned both to make idols and worship to them. How numerous then were, and still are, the idols of the Church of Rome. (*CR*, 10)

On Iona, the archaeologist in her recognized, on a grassy slope leading up from the beach, a row of circular structures and circular stone pavements which she thought could possibly have been the remains of the earliest Columban village and she made a rough sketch when she visited in 1876. She quotes Dean Munro (1594) at length on the subject of Iona and then Pennant, who visited the island in 1772. She speaks also of

> *crumbled churches and churchyards rich in sculpturings which are covered over with ancient vegetation, the roots of which are more like those of trees than of herbs. What brushing and washing has to be done before the work on the stones can be seen, with perhaps the result of finding that they are of the finest art that the Isle of Y has ever chiselled! In such conditions, alas! our countrymen have chosen to let them lie, and are content to let them vanish altogether.* (CR, 18–19)

In venturing to treat of Iona as a second school of Christian art she says that she does not know if the Society of Antiquaries of Scotland's library contains any such classification since, as being only a woman, she was not allowed access to it. In her own attempt to work out a chronological sequence, she distinguishes the earliest tombstones at Iona as being very narrow and she thought that the breadth gradually increased. Christian also thought that the earliest decorations were simple floral interlace. The great man's galley with sail and banner was added rather later, and finally the carvers ventured to depict the famous man himself either as an ecclesiastic or a warrior. Inscriptions were rare, since surely the memory of such a man would never perish. Where no sword was engraved on the slabs she was inclined to believe the tombs could be the graves of nuns and that shears perhaps also designated this. Men on horseback were rare, which she assumed was only natural on an island. She found the prominence of the sword together with other weapons of war; dirk, maul and battle-axe surprising in a monastic burial ground, where one might have expected a cross instead. But it was the sword which was prominent and seemed to be a real representation of the one which had belonged to the dead warrior. Harps and trumpets were also depicted. Male dress was well represented but not female as our forefathers seem to have held the opinion, 'so prevalent in our own day, of the distinct inferiority of the female sex'.

58 *Whithorn, Wigtonshire: 'rubbing' of the 'St Peter' stone (Whithorn 2) (269) (Stirling Libraries)*

Of special note to Christian were the two female graves preserved amongst the tombstones in the still remaining ruins of a nunnery, and being mere women, they were buried apart. One was dedicated to the last prioress of Iona, Anna Maclean, who is represented as attended by angels and is accompanied by a mirror and a comb indicating a female. The inscription which runs down the border of the left side and bottom of this stone reads [*hic jacet d(om)ina anna donal*]*ldi terleti filia quondam priorissa de iona que obiit an(n)o m°d°xl°iii° ei(us) | a(n)i(m)am altissimo [c]o(m)mendam(us)* .... The prioress wears the typical female attire of hood and cloak with a band across the forehead such as was worn by every Highland lady of good family up to about the close of the eighteenth century. Just over half of this stone survives; the missing part bore a representation of the Virgin and Child. The second stone has a simple, tall, slender cross, which Christian supposes to be the tombstone of a nun as it is near the nunnery. Men were thought to be worthy of commemoration whether they were warriors or churchmen whereas women are hardly represented unless very high up in the Church hierarchy. And, alas, the sword is everywhere present as opposed to the figure of the cross.

59 *Soroby, Tiree: 'rubbing' of 'St Michael' cross-shaft (38) (Stirling Libraries)*

At Soriba (Soroby), Tiree, where there was formerly a large monastic institution, she found the shaft of a cross which had later 'served as a tomb-stone' (**59**). 'I found it deeply imbedded in weeds of most vigorous growth, from out of which it required the exertions of a party of five to unearth it.' It would seem from this description that Christian was the first to discover and record this other stone connected with the prioress Anna. The upper portion of the main face of the shaft shows the Archangel Michael fighting with a dragon below which is an inscription: *hic est crux | michael(is) ar|change[l]i dei | anna prior|isa de [y]* 'Here is the cross of Michael, Archangel of God. Anna, Prioress of Iona'. Beneath this stand the figures of Anna and a skeleton flourishing a spade; the Abbess is pulling away and Death has one arm on her robe.

St Martin's Cross on Iona, eluded Christian because of its great height, 20 feet, and 'the upper half of this stately monument' being 'completely shrouded in a thick curtain of hoary lichens'. Why? She was not usually one to be defeated by such minor obstacles. But of Maclean's Cross on Iona she says that her 'rubbing' 'is totally unlike all photographs, that are to be had' for 'in the rubbing it is shown to be exceedingly worn and defaced'.

When she reaches the Priory of Ardchattan on Loch Etive we get a good description of the scenery of the thirty-mile valley:

> Its mountains are lofty and its lake (Loch Etive, a salt-water one) one of the finest in Scotland. At the lower end its beauty is soft and sylvan. At its upper end it pierces into utter desolation and savage grandeur, characteristic of Glencoe, near which it terminates. (CR, 27)

Details of all the bloody battles in the vicinity follow; Edward I of England and the subjugation of the Scots in 1296, a battle in which William Wallace defeated the Irish in the same year near the Pass of Brander, culminating in the battle between the MacDougals and the Campbells in the seventeenth century. How much more interesting this is than a mere catalogue of monuments. In the Priory burial ground she found a stone which 'by frequent tread of feet it is somewhat sunk beneath the common level ground. I have twice found it under rain-water, which had to be baled out before the inscription could be seen. The stone is also broken, and grass is growing through the crack'. She gives Rev Joass's reading of its inscription in Gaelic with an English translation 'Ewen MacDougal, son of Black John'.

The last place in this area is the burying-place of the Campbells of Loch Nell; the 'sacred ruin' resting on

> a green level shore of the lovely Loch Etive, sheltered by venerable trees, and looked down upon by the stupendous Ben Cruachan, whose shadow rests on the calm waters below. Here the early fathers had well chosen their homes, both for life and death.

Who could resist a visit after this description?

At Campbeltown, Kintyre, Christian found a 'goodly cross' in the centre of the town

> on a somewhat lofty pedestal, which, added to the great size of the cross itself, makes it a difficult and almost a dangerous thing to complete a rubbing from it, but this one is truly faithful.

At Finlaggan on Islay she wanted to record a stone on an island in the middle of the loch. When she arrived the water was low due to a drought so that a boat was not absolutely necessary. But a gallant lad volunteered to help the party, which crossed by a plank while he walked alongside. When they came to the end of the plank another was laid down, one always replacing the other until they reached their goal. 'No cringing beggar was our Highland laddie. No! but a true Highland gentleman.' The stones covered the remains of the Lord of the Isles and his darling boy. The larger stone had a sword and was beautifully decorated. Beside it was a much smaller stone with a tiny sword and floral ornaments as on the other one. 'This tells of bitter tears', says the sensitive and caring personality. Then follows a description of the inauguration ceremony of the Lord of the Isles.

From the churchyard at Kil Colmkil (at Lochaline, Morvern) on the mainland, overlooking the Isle of Mull, there was a view considered as perhaps one of the finest in Scotland. 'The view is across the Sound of Mull, and far over that great island itself. Westward it is only limited by the power of the human eye.' She states that 'a beautiful cross' stood 'on a green knoll outside the burying-ground … its base is sunk in a square stone socket, part of a large pedestal', and relates the local custom that when a burial took place, 'the coffin was laid on this pedestal, friends and neighbours standing round, whilst the nearest of kin goes forward to dig the grave'. Responding to this dramatic event in this setting, she surmises 'this scene, with its widespread surroundings of sea and land, if pictured, might make the future of a young artist.'

Within the nave of the ruined church were five stones of 'rarely fine workmanship'.

> *These stones were discovered by me in 1884, being unearthed from a layer of stones and rubbish a foot deep; this being carefully removed, the stones when brushed and washed showed a very beautiful design.* (CR, 45)

One depicted two figures in ecclesiastical robes with twisted bands under a canopy. Others had swords and floral ornaments, and one had a galley with its rigging, in full sail, two men in pointed caps, men on horseback and dogs giving chase to stags amongst floral ornaments. One can sense her excitement.

The section on the 'St. Andrews School' deals entirely with medieval monuments.

Christian's 'Arbroath School' comprises the sculptured stones at St Vigeans, Aberlemno, Glamis, Eassie and Cossans, in Angus; Meigle, Fowlis Wester and the Dupplin Cross, in Perthshire; and the Maiden Stone, at Drumdurno in Aberdeenshire. She considered the collection at Meigle to be very important and it is well represented in her collection, but she was concerned that none of the stones was in its original position, 'but are removed from the churchyard to the sheltering roof of a deserted schoolroom, unpicturesque indeed, but safe', at least from the elements, but 'probably exposed to a danger even greater', which she perceived as 'the parishioners' rights in their proprietorship' being greatly endangered, as had happened with the ancient baptismal font: 'This sacred treasure, the most undoubted property of the Church of Scotland, has been removed and placed in a chapel belonging to the Episcopalians. Surely they are not the heirs of the property of a parish church', she fumes.

Another delightful episode comes in the form of a description of the 'rubbing' taken of the Fowlis Wester cross-slab, Perth and Kinross (**60**). This great carved stone, over 10 feet in height, stood in the middle of the village green.

> *In looking at it with a view to taking a rubbing, I was dismayed at its height, knowing my entire inability to exalt myself, having neither table, chair or*

ladder; but while looking with hopeless gaze, the master of the village inn
joined me, and forthwith, with the utmost zeal, furnished me, not only with one
ladder, but with a pair of them! To complete the scene, the village school having
been dismissed, I was surrounded by the entire assembly of the village youth,
and following them there drew up a carriage and pair alongside of me, and
all these remained for some time spectators of my work. (CR, 55)

This is followed by a detailed description of the famous stone. It would be good
to know the date of this recording but none is given. I include a drawing and a poem,
inspired by an exhibition at the Smith Art Gallery and Museum in Stirling (**61**).

60 *Fowlis Wester, Perthshire: detail of 'rubbing'*
of lower part of reverse of cross-slab (Fowlis
Wester 1) (294) (Stirling Libraries)

Christian Maclagan at Fowlis Wester

Knowledge, she sometimes thinks, is God's great test.
Toiling among the slums or on the stones –
picking her way through Scotland's flesh and bones –
she ponders this, and feels both cursed and blest
by knowledge. God moves in mysterious ways:
gives her inquiry, wealth, a craft to last –
tracing a future from the sculptured past
yet hinders her with bearded antiquaries.
Let Adam girn, as Adam always will:
out here she has her own Society.
God brings a ladder, holds it steady till
she plucks the Pictish apple from the tree.
Children gather, to view her workmanship,
to see the lady climb – and if she'll slip.

61 Christian Maclagan at Fowlis Wester *by James Robertson, with linocut illustration by Owain Kirby (Robertson, 2001).*

62 *Nigg, Easter Ross: 'rubbing' of front of cross-slab (285)*
(Stirling Libraries)

She did 'rubbings' of all faces of the Dupplin cross, which is now displayed in Dunning church, Perth and Kinross (**63**). This great monument is so well known that it needs no description here but I have included the drawing from *ECMS* for comparison. Interestingly, Christian's 'rubbing' does suggest traces of the lettering of an inscription in the top panel of the cross shaft on the reverse, but she did not realise this, commenting only that 'the third panel has been intentionally and thoroughly bereft of all its ornamentation by the chisel' (*CR*, 58). This panel appears blank in the *ECMS* drawing, and it was not until recently that a Roman alphabet

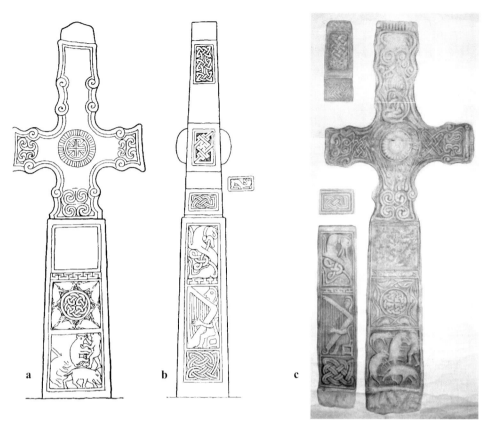

63 *Forteviot, Perthshire:* **c,d** *Christian's 'rubbings' of the faces of the Dupplin Cross (303 & 304) compared with the drawings in* ECMS*:* **a** *front (Fig 334A)* **b** *left side (Fig 334B)* **e** *back (Fig 334C)* **f** *right side (Fig 334D)* (**c,d** *Stirling Libraries*)

inscription was recognised and published, and although it is extremely worn 'this appears to be the result of natural weathering rather than deliberate defacement' (Forsyth 1995).

The 'Fearn Abbey School' covers stones in the north east of Scotland. Shandwick, Nigg, Hilton of Cadboll (then at Invergordon Castle), and Sueno's Stone, at Forres, Moray are all recorded although not all are illustrated amongst the 'rubbings'. Strangely, the far-removed Ruthwell Cross is included here. The reason seems to be that Christian thought that some of its carving (the inhabited vine-scroll) repeated the 'bordering' on the Hilton of Cadboll stone. As it is one of the great early Christian monuments (albeit of Anglian origin) she was 'tempted to include it as it is part of our stone-writ Scottish history'.

The 'rubbing' of the Nigg stone provides an interesting example of Christian's working style (**62**). Her effort is artistic but, as ever, there are notable discrepancies from the original, in some measure due to the nature of the relief carving, with projecting bosses and other elements, which were not compatible to rubbing,

d   e   f

in particular the main panels flanking the cross shaft, which she has, curiously, transposed, and the interlaced beasts in the arms of the cross, which she does not seem to have recognised. Moreover, her version of the carving of the triangular tympanum at the apex deviates considerably from the original. It is clear that her separate sheets were not assembled on the spot, but later, at home, and further checks for accuracy were neither made nor considered necessary for her artistic interpretation.

Christian concludes this section of the book in her inimitable manner:

> *Some may say of these notes that they are too brief, but the greater number will probably think them more than enough; for true it is that the doing of these hundreds of rubbings themselves has proved but a thankless office, and how much more likely that the notes about them will be lightly esteemed.*

followed by a reference to a footnote which reads: 'What if it had been the work of a man?'

64 *Map showing sites where Christian Maclagan made her 'rubbings' of carved stones*[11]

A strangely and sadly prophetic remark, since her 'rubbings' and notes have indeed been generally ignored – but not really for the reason she imagined.

Part II of the book concerns the destruction of the monasteries in whose ruins so many of the carved stones were found. Christian generally disapproved of monasteries as polluted places and 'the homes of shameful immoralities', which are nowhere sanctioned in the Bible. But it is the Earl of Mar who emerges as the chief villain of her piece. He took over Cambuskenneth near Stirling and destroyed it within full view of the royalties enthroned in the castle. Even John Knox exclaimed against Mar's work as a deed of sacrilege. The monks of Cambuskenneth were made homeless and destitute and it was 'the Presbyterian burghers of Stirling kindly cared for them, though there is no note of the pitying alms of royal Maries, Papists as they all were'. Christian's general conclusion is that it was the nobles and not the reformers who were responsible for most of the destruction. They defrauded the Church and the poor of the land; the rest was the responsibility of the wicked English.

In conclusion, the *Catalogue Raisonné* is a mine of information as well as a delightful traveller's guide for those who care to unravel it. It reveals much of Christian's personality, and her passion to record everything she saw. It is, at best, a heterogeneous collection, but it is also a disorganised muddle, full of intriguing, if somewhat irrelevant, digressions. Many of the 'rubbings' it lists can possibly be viewed as works of art; some are charmingly eccentric, but others, which, potentially, could well record lost features of monuments, cannot be relied on to reveal anything because of her general tinkering with the evidence – re-touching the rubbings and employing imaginative interpretation to achieve her final images. It does her no credit to have also copied mistakes from other people's work, the more so as she had a good eye and she should have been more observant in this respect. Her work on the carved stones very much belongs to the old era of the dilettante antiquarian not to the new age of more scientific archaeological recording which was gathering pace towards the end of the nineteenth century.

9   Antiquary, artist and a woman

Christian Maclagan was a fearsome early feminist and with good reason. In the eighteenth century, women of high birth, actresses and some prostitutes had considerable freedom but those from the next lowest station in life, upper middle class and below, generally failed to leave much trace of themselves. In the early-nineteenth century, town life was changing dramatically, bringing much urban distress. Families like that of Christian and her mother realised their social responsibilities very strongly because of a deep and fundamental Christian faith grounded on the Calvinistic principles of John Knox and others.

Christian was possessed of an extremely firm religious faith, based on the literal truth of the Bible. From this she never deviated and this must have been a great strength to her during the turmoils of nineteenth-century scientific discoveries which are strangely nowhere even mentioned in her written work – Darwin's theories do not even merit a note. She was also a stout patriot, believing that the ancient Scots were a brave and noble people who only wanted to defend their homeland from alien and idolatrous invaders such as, in her view, were the Romans. The ancient Scots were ignorant of Christianity but at least they did not worship pagan idols as none were ever found in their dwellings or elsewhere. Their main concern was to defend their homeland against intruders. These views were apparently all her own as she learnt from her father and grandfather all about the Romans but not, as it seems, about ancient British fortifications.

Certainly very sure of herself, she appeared to possess supreme self-confidence. She knew that she had travelled and observed where many others had not. She stresses continually that all her plans and drawings were made on the spot and the measurements were exact, so they cannot be wrong as she took them all herself. Her drawings were faithful, and, if not always artistically finished, they were made on the spot. Yet she was a sensitive and accurate recorder with a keen eye for detail.

Fearless and possessed of a robust constitution, she alone survived when all her siblings succumbed to various illnesses. A great zest for life and adventure were clearly an important part of her personality. Yet she had a warm side to her nature and was a charming hostess. Her inherited wealth was used for social purposes equally with fulfilling her own ambitions in the archaeological field. However she was a woman archaeologist, alone amongst respected male antiquaries and she was determined to be heard. Her eccentric theories go with her strong personality and upbringing. But it must be accepted that she had an inflexible mind-set, which led her to some very wild ideas. Yet, after all, did not the revered archaeologist Gordon Childe's strong Marxist convictions colour his view of the history of mankind?

In dismissing any connection between Druids and stone circles she was probably correct, but then she flies wildly off in the other direction to deny the very existence of stone circles as such with her distinctly odd belief that they are all the foundations of the brochs built by our noble, home-abiding ancestors. From there her beliefs lead her on to assert, with no evidence at all, that the uprights of the circles and dolmens are not bedded deeply into the soil, and she gets even more unreasonable, if possible, when it comes to reconstructions of Stonehenge as a two-storey broch. If it suited her, she was quite prepared to alter evidence to match her theories, almost certainly without realising it. It is perfectly possible to understand how much she must have infuriated fellow antiquaries. But in spite of all this conviction of the correctness of her observations she seems strangely unsure of herself when it comes to standing up in public and reading or speaking to her own papers.

On the positive side, Christian was undoubtedly a pioneer in the study of hillforts, very many of which she visited and measured and sometimes excavated personally, and she was probably the first person to bring all the information on the subject into a usable form. She used the comparative approach with extensive visits abroad and this had not been done before, and some of the monuments she recorded, to the best of her ability, are now degraded or even lost. She was a pioneer populariser of what we call 'Celtic Art', concerned with its possibilities as inspiration to young craftspeople and artists, and the results of her fiercely-guarded secret of taking 'rubbings' were exhibited publicly to that end, to be regarded as works of art in their own right.

Even to the end of her long life she was concerned with the social problems of her time. She was fearless in fighting for women's rights. Her own position as a woman, unworthy of being admitted as a Fellow of the Society of Antiquaries of Scotland riled her throughout her life, and she never lost an opportunity to draw attention to this unjust predicament.

If we are tempted to criticise her 'butterfly' mind let us remember the conditions of the time under which she worked, when collating and arranging such a mass of material and data as she managed to do was not as easy as it is today using computers and electronic aids.

Yet she had a fatal flaw that blighted recognition in her own time in church, artistic and antiquarian circles – she was so certain that she was right that she was unable to understand that others could not accept her views. One can only hope that she died happy in the firm conviction of her own worth and achievements.

Appendix 1   Genealogy

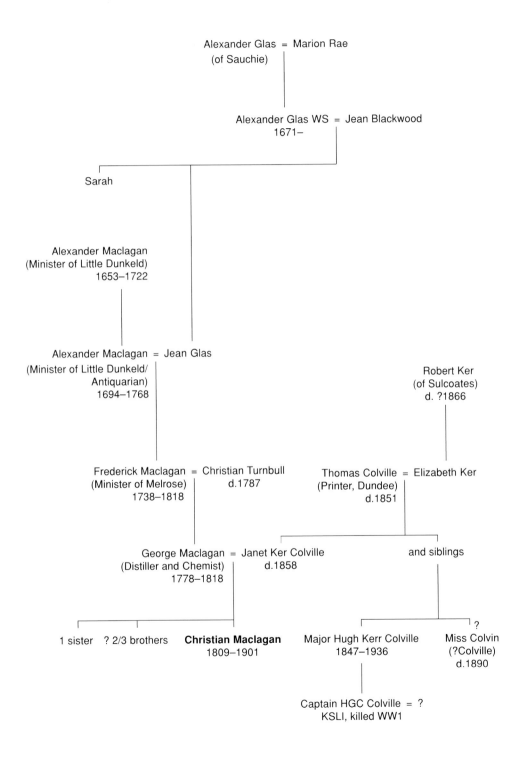

Alexander Glas = Marion Rae
(of Sauchie)

Alexander Glas WS = Jean Blackwood
1671–

Sarah

Alexander Maclagan
(Minister of Little Dunkeld)
1653–1722

Alexander Maclagan = Jean Glas
(Minister of Little Dunkeld/
Antiquarian)
1694–1768

Robert Ker
(of Sulcoates)
d. ?1866

Frederick Maclagan = Christian Turnbull
(Minister of Melrose)   d.1787
1738–1818

Thomas Colville = Elizabeth Ker
(Printer, Dundee)
d.1851

George Maclagan = Janet Ker Colville
(Distiller and Chemist)   d.1858
1778–1818

and siblings

1 sister   ? 2/3 brothers   **Christian Maclagan**
1809–1901

Major Hugh Kerr Colville
1847–1936

?

Miss Colvin
(?Colville)
d.1890

Captain HGC Colville = ?
KSLI, killed WW1

Appendix 2   Prehistoric and Roman Sites mentioned in the text

Modern spelling of place-names is used, with the pre-1975 counties, as this facilitates references to the RCAHMS Inventories

Site	Type	County	OS grid ref	Publication ref
Abbey Craig	Fort	Stirling	NS 809 957	RCAHMS 1963, no 69, 71
Arthur's O' On	Roman Temple	Stirling	NS 879 827	RCAHMS 1963, no 126, 118
Ardifuir	Dun	Argyll	NR 789 969	RCAHMS 1988, no 270, 171–2
Auchenlaich	Roman Fort	Stirling	NN 649 089	See p 37 this volume
Auchinloch	Dun	Stirling	NS 76 79	RCAHMS 1963, no 93, 64
Ballymeanoch	Standing Stones	Argyll	NR 833 964	RCAHMS 1988, no 199, 127–9
Dunmore (Bochastle)	Fort	Stirling	NN 581 076	RCAHMS 1963, no 77, 76
Cairnbaan	Cup-and-Ring Markings	Argyll	NR 838 910	RCAHMS 1988, no 132, 107–8
Coldoch	Dun (multiperiod)	Stirling	NN 679 981	See note 4 this volume
Dumyat	Fort	Stirling	NS 833 973	RCAHMS 1963, no 68, 69–71
Dun a'Bhealaich, Tayvallich	Fort	Argyll	NR 738 871	RCAHMS 1988, no 245, 148
Dun Carloway, Lewis	Broch	Western Isles	NB 190 413	RCAHMS 1985, no 61, 130–1
Dun na Nighinn	Dun	Argyll	NM 849 028	RCAHMS 1988, no 314, 191
Dun Telve	Broch	Inverness	NG 829 172	Ritchie & Ritchie 1998, 154–5
Dun Troddan	Broch	Inverness	NG 833 172	Ritchie & Ritchie 1998, 154–5
East Wemyss	Caves	Fife	NT 342 969–972	RCAHMS 1996b, no 80, 146
Gargunnock, Keir Hill	EIA Homestead	Stirling	NS 706 942	RCAHMS 1963, no 105, 91
Gargunnock, Peel of	Broch (rems of)	Stirling	NS 692 940	RCAHMS 1963, no 191, 179
Kippen	Fairy Knowe	Stirling	unlocated	RCAHMS 1963, no 41, 65
Nether Largie South	Chambered Cairn	Argyll	NR 828 979	RCAHMS 1988, no 19, 48–51
Laws of Monifieth	Fort & Broch	Angus	NO 491 355	Ritchie & Ritchie 1998, 99
The Tappoch, Tor Wood	Broch	Stirling	NS 833 849	RCAHMS 1963, no 100, 85–7
Temple Wood	Stone Circle	Argyll	NR 826 978	RCAHMS 1988, no 228, 138
Tillycoultry	?Cairn	Clackmannan	NS 922 992	See p1 this volume

Appendix 3   Publications of Christian Maclagan

1873a   'On the round castles and ancient dwellings of the Valley of the Forth, and its tributary the Teith', *Proc Soc Antiq Scot*, 9 (1870-72), 29–44.

1873b   'Notes of a Roman sculptured stone recently discovered at Cumbernauld, and of an inscribed stone at Stirling, &c', *Proc Soc Antiq Scot*, 9 (1870-72), 178.

1877   'Notes on the sculptured caves near Dysart, in Fife: illustrated by line drawings of the sculptures' [drawings not by CM], *Proc Soc Antiq Scot*, 11 (1874-76), 107–20.

1875   *The Hill Forts, Stone Circles, and other Structural Remains of Ancient Scotland*, Edmonston and Douglas, Edinburgh.

1881a   'Notice of the discovery of two sculptured stones, with symbols, at Rhynie, Aberdeenshire', *Proc Soc Antiq Scot*, 14 (1879-80), 11–13.

1881   *Chips from Old Stones. By the author of "Hill Forts and Stone Circles of ancient Scotland"*, (Privately and 'anonymously' published) George Waterson and Sons, Edinburgh.

1894   *"What mean these Stones?"*, David Douglas, Edinburgh.

1898   *A Catalogue Raisonné of the British Museum Collection of Rubbings from Ancient Sculptured Stones. A Chapter of Scotland's History etc.* David Douglas, Edinburgh.

Other papers and references

1881   Reference to her presenting three Orkney antiquities (stone scraper, rubber, ancient pottery), *Trans Stirling Natur Hist and Archaeol Soc*, 3 (1880-81), 29.

1882   Reference to her paper on tombstone rubbings from Western Isles, *Trans Stirling Natur Hist and Archaeol Soc*, 4 (1881-82), 19. [read by Ebeneezer Gentleman]

1883   'Sculptured stones of Islay'. *Trans Stirling Natur Hist and Archaeol Soc*, 5 (1882-83), 18, 33. [Paper (6pp) read by David Crystal]

1884   'Fortresses and Dwellings of Ancient People inhabiting the Forth Valley', *Trans Stirling Natur Hist and Archaeol Soc*, 6 (1883-84), 13. [read by Miss Colvin]

1886   'Iona Sculptured Stones' *Trans Stirling Natur Hist and Archaeol Soc*, 8 (1885-86), 15. [(13pp) read by Miss Colvin]

1890   'Rubbings of Sculptured stones in the east and west of Scotland', *Trans Stirling Natur Hist and Archaeol Soc*, 12 (1889-90), 85–7. [read by Miss Colvin]

1892   'Rubbings from Ardcahattan Priory', *Trans Stirling Natur Hist and Archaeol Soc*, 13 (1890-92), 70–4. [Mr R Kidston read and explained her notes.]

1895   'The recently discovered sculptured stones at St Andrews', with comments by George Lawson. *Trans Stirling Natur Hist and Archaeol Soc*, 17 (1894-95), 54–5.

Notes

1 Born 1825, daughter of Robert Colvin D.D., one of eight children. Died of pleurisy at Ravenscroft in 1890. Her mother was a daughter of the manse and two of her brothers went into the ministry.

2 It is recorded that a photograph accompanied her note on the Roman slab from [Arniebog] Cumbernauld (1873b, 178), but this seems to be the sole instance of Maclagan's association with photography.

3 East Coldoch is currently under excavation by a team from Durham University (*Current Archaeology Handbook 2001–2*). East Coldoch (NS 703–986) is a part of the Roman Gask frontier in Perthshire built by the Romans in AD80, 40 years before Hadrian's Wall and 60 years before the Antonine wall. This excavation is a long term project looking at the native side of the equation. It is a multi-period defended enclosure whose occupation is thought to extend into the Roman period.

4 This is Nether Largie South Cairn (RCAHMS 1988. no 19, 48–51).

5 Today one has to ignore the caravan site.

6 Last wolf in Scotland shot *c*1760.

7 Christian visited all six caves with Dr Stuart and her friend Mr Drummond and she refers to the plates of the late lamented Sir J Y Simpson, whose drawings of the carvings were used to illustrate the paper. These are crudely drawn and are not to scale. Neverthless the account is well worth a read as it records many non-archaeological details of the caves which were to be seen at the time.

8 The catalogue numbering of the 'rubbings' and locations is also available in the British Library Catalogue of Manuscripts under: Add. 34798 and Add. 35165A–35165D.

9 For confirmation see *CR*, app 2, 79

10 Nevertheless, the following acknowledgement, probably referring to the so-called 'map', appears in the Society's proceedings: 'Miss Maclagan has also sent for exhibition a large drawing of the sculpturings of cups and concentric circles on the Auchnabreck Rocks.' (*PSAS*, 9 (1870-72), 179).

11 Based on information gleaned from Maclagan's *Catalogue Raisonné* with modern or amended spelling.

Bibliography

Allen, J R and J Anderson 1903 *The Early Christian Monuments of Scotland*, 3 parts, Society of Antiquaries of Scotland, Edinburgh (reprinted 1993, 2 vols, Pinkfoot Press, Balgavies, Angus).

Bain, A 1965 *Education in Stirlingshire from the Reformation to the Act of 1872*, London.

Chalmers, P 1848 *The Ancient Sculptured Monuments of the County of Angus*, Bannatyne Club, Edinburgh.

Chambers, W 1864 *A History of Peeblesshire*, Edinburgh.

Christison, D 1898 *Early Fortifications in Scotland*, Edinburgh.

—— 1906 'Report on the Society's excavations of forts on the Poltalloch Estate, Argyll', *Proc Soc Antiq Scot*, 39 (1904-05), 259–322.

Collins, P 2002 *Banvard's Folly.* (The man with N-Ray eyes)

Cordiner, C 1788 and 1795 *Remarkable Ruins, and Romantic Prospects, of North Britain*, London.

Feachem, R W 1955 'Fortifications', in F T Wainwright (ed), *The Problem of the Picts*, 66–86, Edinburgh.

Feachem, R W 1977 *A Guide to Prehistoric Scotland*, London.

Forsyth, K 1995 'The Inscriptions on the Dupplin Cross', in C Bourke (ed) *From the Isles of the North: early Medieval Art in Ireland and Britain*, 237–44, HMSO, Belfast.

Gordon, A 1726 *Itinerarium Septentrionale: or a Journey through most of the Counties of Scotland and those of the north of England*, London.

Harding, D 1990 'Atlantic Round Houses', in I Armit (ed), *Beyond the Brochs,* Edinburgh University Press, Edinburgh

La Lomand 1853 *Statistique Historique,* Administration du Département de Morbihan, Vannes.

La Marmora, A 1839 *Voyage en Sardaigne*, vols 1 and 2, Paris, vol 3, 1857, Turin.

Lukis, W C 1875 *A Guide to the Principal Chambered Barrows etc. of South Brittany*, Ripon.

Mahé, J 1825 *Antiquités de Morbihan.*

Mair, C 1990 *Stirling: the Royal Burgh,* John Donald and Stirling Public Library

MacKie, E W 1975 *Scotland: An Archaeological Guide*, Faber and Faber, London.

McCutcheon, B 1986 *Stirling Observer 150 years on,* Stirling Observer.

Muir, T S 1855 *Ecclesiological Notes on Some of the Islands of Scotland*, David Douglas, Edinburgh.

Pennant, J 1774 *A Tour in Scotland and Voyage to the Hebrides; MDCCLXXII*, Chester.

RCAHMS (Royal Commission on the Ancient and Historical Monuments of Scotland)

—— 1963 *Stirlingshire: An Inventory of the Ancient Monuments*, HMSO, Edinburgh

—— 1985 Ritchie, G and M Harman *Argyll and the Western Isles*, 'Exploring Scotland's Heritage' Series, HMSO, Edinburgh.

—— 1988 *Argyll: An Inventory of the Monuments*, vol 6, *Mid Argyll and Cowal: Prehistoric and Early Historic Monuments*, HMSO, Edinburgh.

—— 1999 [Ritchie, J N G and I Fraser] *Pictish Symbol Stones: an illustrated gazetteer*, Edinburgh.

—— 1996a Shepherd, I *Aberdeen and North East Scotland*, 'Exploring Scotland's Heritage' Series, HMSO, Edinburgh.

—— 1996b Walker, B and G Ritchie *Fife, Perthshire and Angus*, 'Exploring Scotland's Heritage' Series, HMSO, Edinburgh.

Ritchie, A and J N G Ritchie 1998 *Scotland*, Oxford Archaeological Guides, Oxford.

Ritchie, J N G 1998 *Recording Early Christian Monuments in Scotland*, Groam House Museum Trust, Rosemarkie.

Robertson, J 2001 *Stirling Sonnets* (illustrated by O Kirby), Kettillonia, Kingskettle. ('Christian Maclagan at Fowlis Wester', p14)

St Joseph, J K S 1978 'The camp at Durno, Aberdeenshire, and the Site of Mons Graupius', *Britannia*, 9, 271–87.

Spano, G 1854 *Memoria sopra Nuraghi della Sardegna*, Cagliari.

—— 1871 *Paleoetnologia sarda ossia l'età preistorica segnata dai monumenti che si travano in Sardegna*, Cagliari.

Steel, F A and G Gardiner 1911 *The complete Indian Housekeeper and Cook*, London

Stirling Public Libraries 1909 *The Industries of Stirling and District*, compiled from extracts from *The Stirling Observer*.

Stuart, J (ed) 1856–1867 *Sculptured Stones of Scotland*, 2vols, Spalding Club, Aberdeen (i) and Edinburgh (ii).

Index

P

Paulo Latini 71, 74
passage graves 79
Pennant, Thomas 82, 86, 93
Phoenicians 65
photography 87
Pictish symbols 91
Piggott, Stuart 26
Political reform 8
Poltalloch 37
Pope, Miss 88

Q

Queen Victoria 11

R

Rhynie 23, 86
River Carron 31
Rome 25, 27, 69, 79, 91
roofing of brochs 67
runes 92
Ruthwell Cross 92, 100

S

Salmond, Mr J 43
Sardinia 19, 25, 26, 27, 65
Sardinian Antiquarian Society 73
Seville 91
Shandwick 100
Shetland 18
Silbury Hill 58
Silonus 74
Simpson, Sir James Young 14, 17, 23, 24, 34
Soroby, Tiree 94
souterrains 76, 79
Southesk, Earl of 92
Spalding Club 86
Spano, Giovanni 70
St Andrews 96
St Columba 92
St Joseph, Professor 45
St Martin's Cross 94
St Ninian 92
St Vigeans 96
St Vigeans, 'Drosten Stone' 23

S continued

Stenness, stones of 58
Stirling
    Archaeological Society 34
    Broad Street 6
    burghers of 103
    Field Club 9
    Mary Kirk 14
    Mission Sunday School 13
    Natural History and Archaeological Societ 9
    Old Bridge 7
    Pitt Terrace 11
    School Board, election 13
    School of Arts 9
    Smith Art Gallery and Museum 67, 97
    St Mary's Wynd 8, 13, 17
    Tract Enterprise 10
    Wallace Monument 13, 35
    Working conditions 7
Stokes, Margaret 21
stone avenues 74
stone rows 76
Stonehenge 57
Stuart, Dr John 17, 22, 45, 87
Stukeley, William 26
Sueno's Stone, Forres 100

T

Table des Marchands 76
Tacitus 45
talayot 65
Tappock 31, 63
Tayvallich 18, 41
Tillicoultry 35
Torwood 63
transport, methods of 7
Turner, Christina 15

W

Wallace, William 95
Wemyss Caves 85
wheelhouse 83
White Caterthun 62, 91
Whithorn 92

ΧΡΙΣΤΙΑΝ

The Pinkfoot Press

Balgavies, Forfar, Angus DD8 2TH

inbox@pinkfootpress.co.uk